The Black Book of the Master Mind Part 3

By, David K Drews

Hope is For the Hopeless

Corporations, churches, media personalities, schools, political and other organizations frequently want **your hope,** and **your trust** to be with them.    All the great "I am's" are to be isolated, mocked, and persecuted.    Many people will tell you it's impossible to succeed, at least without them.    People suck up to these "authorities" in hopes of getting a better life, and get burned.

Those mentioned above have long since abandoned the Bible, the Constitution of the United States, reason, competition, and individuality, for collectivism under "elite" rule.

Today the elites push "global governance."
Yes, even many churches.    Churches that don't
support the elites are labeled "underground" or
said to have prosperity doctrines (as if that's
really bad).

Keep in mind, while you create your businesses,
and run your life, the "elites" and all their
workers know psychology, sociology,
persuasion, hypnosis, street hypnosis,
negotiation, and other knowledge that help
them slowly tighten their grip on every aspect
of life for everyone on planet earth.    "Social
skills" are their main weapon and lure.    All
forms of capitalism are the enemy.    Many
people pose as opponents of the elites and
seem to delay, "accidentally" screw up, and
even betray their supporters.

Keep in mind, many people are apathetic,
double minded, and/or ready to make
accusations against family and friends, in
exchange for kudos and recognition from some
tyrant.    How do you know the republicans you
talk to don't suck up to tyrants behind your
back?    How do you know the CCINO
(conservative Christian in name only) don't
spread rumors about you because you want a

better life?   You're not asking permission from perverters of justice or any other liar to improve your life.

It's not your fault most "leaders" shit-can their moral compass and principles.   Don't make the mistake of thinking public schools will ever teach and encourage entrepreneurship, capitalism, transparency, the Bill of Rights, economics, or history.   This stuff has been rewritten, redefined, mocked, and manipulated by and for "elites."

Besides, you don't want the government to start trying to teach some of these things anyway. Government has a tendency to warp, and destroy things it gets its hands on.

You can't get the benefits of good by using evil methods. I tell you this because good people sometimes try to get good results from doing what they believe some corrupt person has done.

Think about what I'm saying.   Don't let the media think for you.   The news media will not cast their "superiors" in a bad light, until after the election is over or until after the scandal of a law is passed.   Don't waste time pouring through newspapers and other media looking for journalists to cast you, your MasterMind, your candidate, or your faith in a positive light. Sure, broken clocks are right twice a day. Cancel your newspaper subscription, and do something more productive with your time and energy.

Watch Kafka, and They Live, before watching for the masses news.

People **say** there is no hope and to act like total spineless wimps.    Don't listen to them!

Listen to me.

You need the right kind of peer pressure from a MasterMind to avoid becoming a statistic!

God says "Hard workers get rich." Listen to that.

Patriots say "The answer to 1984 is 1776. Listen to that.

Positive peer pressure, God's Word, and 1776 are available to every one of over six billion people on this planet.    Don't seek approval from tyrants, their spokespersons on TV, or idiots.    Yes, you are most assuredly going against the grain.    Even if you say nothing in public about your plans, the RINO's, LINO's, and "non-judgmental" religious types will chatter, and contort their faces.


## Gather Your Tools

Contrary to what "experts" who are supposedly on your side say, you do still have a lot of weapons, and tools at your disposal.

First, you have your attention.    Pay attention to what you want.    Pay attention to what you respect and admire.    Don't pay attention to your enemies, as they expect attention, praise, legitimacy, and for you to work for them for free.    People who want you under their thumb will just try to confuse you.    Kill your TV, and breathe life into your dreams.

Second, whether you live in the U.S. or not you are born free.    You have rights.    Neither the Federal Reserve or Ivy League politicians gave you any rights.    Those people want to take your rights away.

So be free in your mind.    Reject unfair laws. Feel free to criticize corrupt politicians, and "superiors", if you choose.    Obviously, you don't want to drink their kool aid. You don't have to think the way your government professor says you should. Free yourself from sales talk, empty campaign talk, and find the best options for yourself.

Third, you have common sense. Utilize it. In the past our real leaders warned us of subversion, fallacy, scheming, debauchery, immorality, false teachers, irresponsibility, and socialism. We used to be warned as children of pied pipers. Today, real leaders and teachers are few and far between here where I live. But, seek and you will find.

If it hurts, maybe you shouldn't do it. If it's not real food, don't eat it. If it is not a comedy movie, don't try it if it's illogical or unreasonable.

Just as no one owes you anything, you don't owe anyone else anything.

Fourth, you have your memory. The "elites" and all their disciples tell us to forget what they said an hour ago, and to obey, and to accept feces as gold. Remember the schemes used against you. If you choose to forget what will prevent the same scam a second time?

Definitely forgive, but don't become a doormat or a lamp shade.   Remember not to bet the farm when expectations are irrational. Sometimes the scandal is what's legal.

Remember all types of things that really work and are helpful.   Find new ideas and tips that are helpful.   Obviously, you will want to remember friends, how to get customers, where to get the best deal on anything you may need, how to do a SWOT analysis, ways to improvise, and many other things.

Fifth, you have (hopefully) your earning power. Increase your earning capacity if you can, by learning valuable skills.   Outsource small tasks. Invest in any type of tool you firmly believe will help you make more money.   Don't do things that jeopardize your earning power.

Sixth, you have your network.   A person wrongly demonized by some politician, reporter, pastor, teacher, or anybody might actually be a like-minded friendly person who stood up for himself.   Anyone opposed to your success, and bliss may demean or socially isolate, bait you, or worse.   All your real friends must understand this.   A potential spouse must understand.   Your MasterMind must understand.    If one does not, then he will be the person who turns against you and your friends (and for a pittance).    Yes, like Judas.

Seventh, you have a Master Mind group (MMG).    At least you should be in one soon. Your Master Mind needs to be closed to outside influences and negativity.    Figure out how to turn negativity into good productive work.    In your MMG, you need members with skills, knowledge, and resources you do not.    Your members should have similar goals.    The people in your Master Mind have to abide by your group's basic rules and be willing to help each other for money, for trade, or for free.

Your MMG needs to operate in a spirit of unity and harmony.

Eighth, you have your cell phone, PC, software, physical tools, physical equipment, cash, real estate, and specialized knowledge that you can use to improve your life, your customer's life or to reach any goal.

Ninth, you hopefully have mobility.    You hopefully have a vehicle, and the ability to relocate and travel should you want to.

Tenth, you have your word (and credit, and reputation).

Eleventh, you have God.    God can move mountains.    God gave you the power and ability to control yourself, animals, and more. You do have the power to watch TV, gossip and drink rum but those things only get you so far.

Choose MasterMind members who minimize your weaknesses and have the tools, knowledge, contacts, and assets you lack. Plan how you approach potential MMG members.    Be honest with the potential member as well as yourself.    Do not involve dolts, phony friends, crooks, or sleaze in any aspect of your life or MasterMind.    Avoid people who hover, pry, or reinterpret everything you say. Relocate if you must. Definitely don't lose your right to keep and bear arms.


## Make a Plan

Let's forget about politics and big sister for a bit. Let's talk about reaching your financial goal, which is not to be a statistic, but someone with at least a comfortable life.

Shut out all the bullshit judgment, and noise, and opinion and start saving money.    If you don't have a job or even better, a business, then get one or two.    Use your savings to invest in the investments of your choice and/or a business of your own that you control.

If the income from your job doesn't pay all the bills, look into doing odd jobs, contract work, and so forth, to keep the lights on.    Grow your network without flat out asking for work. Start to improve your performance, appearance, punctuality, and be consistently reliable at your work. Be the guy who never complains.    Then ask for overtime or a promotion.    Don't become a spammer, scammer, or your company's arm pit.    Don't listen to new "friends" who tempt you to be a pest.

I typed up a Kindle eBook called "Save $1000 per Month."    You could save more than that, depending on your income, and how hard you're willing to search for deals.    Truthfully, I am pretty proud of the mindset section of that eBook.

Have your Master Mind look at your budget, if

you so desire.    Budget conscious and minimalist MMG members can help you cut spending.    You can use hypnosis on each other to quit smoking, enjoy working, avoid overeating, and etc.    To borrow a line from Robert Kiyosaki, you want assets, not a doodad or a luxury you can't afford.

If you don't have the cash to buy real estate or to start a big business, look for employment or self-employment, like:

- Handyman

- House/pet sitter

- SEO consultant

- Information marketing

- Entertainer (including screenplay writing)

- Day care

- Run a food kiosk

- Tutor (or other type of instructor)

- Construction (of mountain retreats, panic rooms and etc.)

- Affiliate marketer (but to do this you need sufficient traffic, continuing amazing content and a big opt-in list)

- Programmer

- Driver (look into Hazmat)

- Ethical hacker

- Office or clinic cleaner

- Other specialized cleaning.

- Private investigations.

- A small security company.

- A branding or marketing consultant, etc.

There are lots of jobs you can do for extra money.    Look at the quick cash ideas page at http://.www.renegadeuniversity.net.    I added several ideas recently.

The thing you really want is a scalable business. A scalable business saves so much of your time after the business is built.

Info products have perfect scalability.    EBooks and audios can sell long after they are published.   You don't have to print the books yourself.   If you had the equipment, you could hire a person to make the physical books, that's still scalability.   You do have to generate traffic and start a buzz though.

Software offers scalability.   You can sell downloads and/or CD-ROMs.   After the operation is up and running, you can outsource customer service. Of course, you'll need to know a programming language.   Learning to program takes time.   People might call you crazy for teaching yourself C, MySQL, java, etc. Learn a programming language anyway.

You could design any physical product you invent or redesign, and hire workers to make them in your town, or you can outsource manufacturing.

Stick to products with strong demand.   Keep in mind the economy is just limping along. Even if people would buy it, could they buy it (your product)?   Just like you'd look at a 10K and 10Q for a stock purchase, you'd want to market research before starting a business.

A good idea would be to look at Coursera dot org or MIT Open Courseware and learn entrepreneurship, for free.

Get in a MMG or start a MMG where at least one member has experience in your field, or at least has started at least one business.

The Gold Rush is On - What Can You Sell the Gold Miners?

What can you sell app developers?    What can you sell into any crazed or hot market?    It's the same as entrepreneurs in the California gold rush selling tools, clothes, and supplies to gold miners.    Not all the entrepreneurs were gold miners.

Let me list some hot niches you could sell into: MLM's, affiliate marketing, job searching, higher education, specialized training, eBook authors, fitness, organic food, and organic supplements, improving credit scores, and the list goes on. What could you sell to entrepreneurs or their growth hackers?

Ok, I have introduced you to some ideas that will get you started.    Now, let's get the right kind of peer pressure so we'll follow through on our plans.

Who to Recruit to Your Master Mind

Let's start with Gordon Gekko.    He wanted guys who were "poor, smart, and hungry."

No, lol, let's start with you.    What skill(s) do you lack?    Who can you find to teach you? What do you have to offer your MM members?

Have you met a person who brings out the absolute best performance in you or in others? Invite that person.

How about a person who achieved what you want to do also? Choosing to model a successful person is a good idea.

A good MMG member would be a good accountability partner.

I read, I believe in Inc. magazine, that major tech companies hire outstanding talent, contagious personalities, and experience from other big startups, even if there is no clearly defined role for the employee.    Some readers of this eBook are now a little angry, saying "wth?" but, I believe this is a good way to recruit some of your Master Mind.

Another type of person to recruit is a person who consistently acts, and holds to his grand vision for their life. Clinging to your vision takes courage.   If you're impressed by the little train, and how he or she sticks to it, there is a potentially good member.   People are really driven by their BHAGs (big hairy audacious goals).

A person who can sell superbly, online, on the phone, and face to face could be really helpful, if they will teach you to sell. Such a person, if they are lucid and well-reasoned, can teach you NLP.   Not just tell you, but really make you proficient.

Recruit a person who sees opportunity, especially in negative change, (even crisis) like we have today in the U.S.   You could sell health insurance.   You could attempt to supply the government with any product or service you can. You could sell to preppers, political debaters, and activists of all sorts. You can buy real estate, businesses, business assets, and/or shares in a panic.

You can recruit an army of one.   You can recruit one man think tanks.   You may have to search for these people.   But, you need to become one too.

## Where to Recruit for Your Master Mind

In the first Black Book of the Master Mind, I have a list of places to recruit for your MMG.

At the top of the list, a Yahoo Group, run by me, called IndependentWealth.   There are numerous other forums online too.   At the major business forums, people start Master Minds all the time.   After the tasks and short mission of these MMG's have been completed, you can cherry pick from the best members. You can bring to your main, permanent MMG the best talent you can find, and of course all the lessons, data, and knowledge from the old MMG's battles.

You can **cherry pick** from your forums and offline organizations, as well as other people's groups.

You can attend local networking events, and recruit a person.

Another idea is to join Neil Strauss' organization, called "The Society."

Recruiting a graduate of the Leadership Institute, in Alexandria, Virginia or another superior specialized school may be good. Good campaign workers can make excellent marketers, and vice versa.

You can find MMGs, and people suited for your MMG at Meetup dot com.

Look at a business that is shutting its doors permanently.   An employee at a soon to be defunct business may see what business comes next, and grasp the lessons of their employer's failure.   A smart person will see what replaces the old business.

Don't deal with a person, with a good income or a low income, who won't make a budget or manage cash at all.   Don't feel bad for them. Keep those people out of your Master Mind group give them no part in your finances or your business's finances.

Avoid people who fully reject Dave Ramsey, the Wall Street Journal, or any common sense preaching teacher or guru.   If the person insists on dealing with scam businesses, and criminals only, you have to avoid them.   Some of those idiots will tirelessly bang their heads against the wall trying to win with scams.    If you can't snap them out of their trances, leave them.    If you reject this, I'm sure you trust politicians to play fast and loose with your future, and your right to self-defense.

You want peer pressure from achievers, and contributors to society, rather than the leeches.


Conspiracies

As I wrote in part 2 of this series, the downfall of the U.S. was planned long ago.    Steering the U.S. over the cliff will make things equitable for the rest of the world, a professor told his class, in 1994.

After you read the following, you'll see the facts fit.

- We are trained to phrase our affirmations and hypnosis in a positive way.    Telling yourself, "Never, ever do that!" has to be more effective than trying to formulate a mush mouth positive statement.    Sure, 3/4 of our parents overcorrected us with "no's" and negative reinforcement.

Experiment on yourself when you use self-hypnosis and see if using "negative" affirmations move you.

I honestly think this positive phrasing stuff is conspiracy, made to make Americans dumb, gullible, and malleable.

- Don't be a perfectionist.   Do sloppy performances win big money?   Does sloppy cleaning and maintenance pass inspection? Does being a perfectionist have to keep you from getting things done? I say no.   If you were a perfectionist, would you ever practice your craft, sport, or whatever? Yes, and you'd practice and learn the lessons via the mistakes that are necessary to become excellent.

- We are trained to watch TV and obey it. Frequently, we humans try to please mouth pieces, ambush facilitators, mockers, and critics we see and hear on all media.   How much do these programs help you make money, get in shape, or help victims of their onslaught? Are you happy with the politicians and society TV has given us?   As a society, we care too much about the opinions of fools and evil people.

- Our "superiors" act as if genuine achievement

doesn't boost self-esteem.   It does.   Kill your TV and accomplish something.   Many kids in this country are apathetic and unmotivated because of brainwashing, and constant attacks on their values, and families. Don't stop and seek an idiot's opinion or approval if you can avoid it.

Your next accomplishments don't have to be real grandiose.   Just get your to-do lists done every time you make one.

- Individualists, entrepreneurs, and people who stand up for themselves are frequently isolated, mocked, hoodwinked, and falsely accused. "Right wingers" who insist on putting the elite's nonsense in their heads via news and church, will scatter when their genuine leaders are struck. (Think of Sarah Palin, Ron Paul, Fred Thompson, and even Mitt Romney). They are easily divided against each other and themselves.   If you are divided against yourself, you'll find things will not work out.

- Our "authorities" tell us we're not and can't hope to be special.   Horse pucky, you have to be special to succeed, thrive, to get suitable companions, and clients. Commie babes, who can be very hot, that want an obscure worker someplace, are pretty rare.    Enhance positive traits that make you special.

- They say you have to go to college. No you don't.    Many billionaires quit or did not attend college. You can Google your education, like Sean Parker says.    You can read how-to's. You can experiment on your own.    You can search for instructional videos on youtube. You can go to a seminar.    Professors at your local college won't approve.

- When professors (and others) drop a truth bomb, they will immediately put the sh*t back in the horse or sugarcoat the facts so people don't "turn negative" or panic.    Be the special kind of person that pulls the poison pill right out of all the tasty stuff and says, "Remember this?" The teacher or whoever can still say they told you the truth, although they used red herrings, smoke in mirrors, or said not to repeat this, etc. to cover the facts.

- People are told the government can and will take care of them.    Like 19th century Native Americans?    Like bank customers in Cyprus? Like the famous whistleblowers of recent history? Like retirement account owners in Argentina?    Like 86 year old military veterans in the U.S. that need heart surgery?    Like any convenient whipping boy in all history?

- Your English teachers doubtlessly told you cursing in writing is always bad.    Be realistic, an edgy headline, blurb, or title will attract eyeballs. "Get organized" is pretty how hum. But being told to "get your shit together" gets more attention from your target audience.

- Alpha males are cast in a bad light by academics.    In school we were told to work for or sell services to alpha males.    It's the alpha males that make the sick money.    As bad as many of our schools and colleges are, why listen to anti-alpha male nonsense?

- We are told not to get angry.    If you get angry, you might make difficult decisions, and improve your life.

Oh, and don't pay attention to the Georgia Guide Stones.    Google the Georgia Guide Stones some time.

Get your MasterMind or the mentors in your MasterMind to **kick your ass, take logical steps towards your goals**, stay up late, face fears, and even multitask, if you must to get things done.

Even if another writer or some shitty "superior" of yours bombards you with, "it's impossible! You can't even be serious! What money do you represent?" or other negative attacks, **do what you can with what you have**.

Do notice, and point out exactly how hypocritical your phony friend is.


The Cons

But, who are these powerful people in the shadows that conspire against us? How do they operate? I'll tell you a little about them. You have doubtlessly seen first-hand or suspected some authority of some type act like a learning disabled punk one moment, and then a genuine compassionate leader the next. On campus is where you find many of them. But there are also churches, businesses, and government agencies.

It takes a lot of ability to con large numbers of people and still win elections and votes of confidence, and maintain decent PR. Divide and conquer is their first rule. Attempt to divide your adversaries and do not allow your

Master Mind, your marriage, or any other union to divided, or the con artists win.

Don't let your foes dictate sh*t to you, make you repeat yourself, or put words in your mouth.

Why does it seem it's really a one party system here in the U.S.?   Because the D's have eyes and ears in everything Republican. EVERYTHING.    In your school and church, D's and R's were treated differently.    This is true almost everywhere.    I knew a lot of young, and old R's that were and are submissive to the Left via their church or employer, etc.

Cons will lie to you, and lie more, when you catch them lying.    The enemy is the person lying to you, not the personality-type the media rails against.    The enemy says you should pay for the crime the person next to you committed.    Even if we get RINO's back in the White House, I fear we'll see an increase in government bullying.

The cons know pop, and street psychology cold. When you hear them speak platitudes, keep in mind who they are.

If you come in contact with a politician, you need to determine if they're a John the Baptist, or if they want to go to D.C. to nail Herrod or his daughter.    The latter two are probably useless to you.    John the Baptist types are a tiny minority.    You may want to appreciate them because their peers hate them.

Politics in the U.S. is centered on bribery, and lobbying.

All the Risk. All the Adversity

We tried and failed, some people will tell me. Try again, I say.    Try a different approach. Shut out negative and hyper optimistic opinion. Spend some time with your MasterMind.    Do some group hypnosis or guided visualization, or a brainstorming session.    Scrape the barnacles off your ship.    Weed out informants and people who won't follow instructions.

What seems like a logical action to move closer to your goal? Getting a subscription to Guru Focus? Running stock screeners and researching companies you think you like?    Picking an analyst's brain?    Reviewing you budget and bank records? Looking for investors for your next business?

There are lots of side projects you can start.    It may not be entertaining, but you can start a small venture, and try to get a sale.    Like I said, at my site I have a list of fast cash ideas.    Use them.    The "executive" job will never manifest.

If you at all a self-starter, you can take a vaporous idea, flesh it out, test it, contemplate it and see if you have a viable idea.    90% of businesses fail, 99% of affiliate marketers fail, 98% of MLM's fail.    Did the ones who succeeded not try?    Failing at a business doesn't make you a failure.    If you can manage the risk, why wouldn't you go for it?    I know I have told you some negative things in this book. But instill in yourself a buoyant attitude.

Gain an understanding of your investment vehicle(s) and businesses.    You can usually correct course or make adjustments after you launch.    Do the work you feel will help you overcome the odds.    Be wary of trolls.    Be wary of "advisors" who get paid whether you succeed or fail.

If you are currently in college, you have around

you people who will knife you and play games with you.    Be wary of these crooks and give them nothing.    When their superiors request your presence or some favor, lower the boom on them.    They despise small business people, investors, and anyone who dares to outshine the master.    Keep in mind, life immediately following graduation is frequently found to be miserable.

If you can't afford to lose any money on a business, find a second job.    Be a pet sitter. Work behind a counter on a night shift.    If it's allowed, work on your projects then.

If you are interested in this stuff, don't just read passively.    Make a to-do list.


MasterMind Rules and Regulations

Tony Robbins says people with fewer rules are happier.    I have seen much firsthand evidence of this.    If you can't do anything because of all the rules, you have a problem.    If you feel bad for not following a stupid rule, what good does it do?    If your choices are vastly limited because of rules, beliefs, threats of punishment, and low self-esteem, this is counterproductive.

I'm not for total anarchy.    Follow the Golden Rule and run your MasterMind in a genuine spirit of unity and harmony, and I'll predict awesome results.

Anyway, don't bring in socialist thought, crime, fraud, a foreign agenda or influence into your MasterMind.    Don't stomp into a MasterMind and become the thought cop, the insane cousin, the tattle tale, the tyrant, the moocher, the hazer, the slanderer, a sewer rat, or any one too militant about some unrelated cause or person. People do those things and act holier than thou about it.    Of course they can't acknowledge you about it either, that's not in progressive church dogma.    Vandalizing your car is OK.

You should insist that you and your MasterMind follow the Golden Rule and operate in a spirit of unity and harmony.    Trolls will want to influence you, and your MMG.

In my MasterMind, we have one more rule: no complacency.    As Tony Robbins says, "If you're green you grow, when you're ripe you rot." Always be growing and practicing CANI, constant and never ending improvement.    If reach a major goal, get going on a new challenging goal before you become complacent.

If someone has to read five hundred pages of rules and nonsense to be in your MasterMind I see bankruptcy , depression, and looking over your shoulder in your future.

Don't drag the chatter at your job into your MasterMInd. Unless your job is pretty awesome.    Don't bring the social regulations of your school into your MasterMind.    Find the atmosphere and mindset that work for your particular MasterMind.    Why recreate what you want to be free of?    The dictates of the bosses at work or school work for your bosses' bosses, not you.


More Things Your MasterMind Should Do

Ask your MMG these questions:

- Are you working on your dreams today?

- How much closer to your island are you?

- Did you learn anything useful today?

- Did you encounter any energy vampires today?

- Did you get _____ started (or finished)?

- What conspiracy theory did you hear today?

- Did you experience anything awesome today?

- What kind of juice or smoothie did you make today?

- Did you haul buckets or build a pipeline?

- Did you eliminate any time or money wasters?

- Did you face any fears today?

- How did you learn that so fast?

- Did you talk to any interesting people today?

- Did you find yourself thinking in _____ (language) today?

Tell your MasterMind you are each other's eyes and ears.    Be alert.    Be ready for anything, including opportunity.    Be wary of trolls and cons. Cover each other's blind spots.    Other authorities may have failed.    But not you or your MasterMind.    Sloth, excuses, and bad decisions have no place in your life or MasterMind.    Say this: if it's to be, it's up to me.

Remind each other who you are.    Tell yourselves you're the revolutionaries, the new Skull and Bones, or the new version of any organization you choose.    This could rally your MMG, and remind your members of their mission.

Make each day awesome.    Consistently deferring awesomeness to the future, to someday, pretty much go against what my MMG believes.    You obviously cannot make a billion dollars yesterday, but there is much you could do today.    Asking the above questions and questions that come from reading personal development books or audios or experiencing awesomeness will help prevent you from kicking the can down the road.

The elites play the delay game on you.    Don't

copy them, and delay your personal happiness for yourself.

Decide what the best opportunities are for you and then either execute right away or make a plan.    If you are looking for capital gains, I'd choose a growth stock or an option over a large mutual fund any day.    Search for the best opportunity.    Look past sales talk. Be honest with yourself. The first deal you find may not be it.    Learn what you need to.

Keep in mind most plans fail.    It's better to have one or two plans though.

Get your mentors in your Master Mind to walk you through new thinking and behaviors.    You may need to move through blocks. You need to choose your own feelings and beliefs about anything and everything to really get to the next level. Identify any obstacles and self-defeating beliefs and begin working to overcome or change them.    Schools and companies frequently avoid training people, so you may have to train yourself.

One writer says to "create your life all day long."    You can't create and procrastinate at the same time.    Use the power of right now.

Even if you're not young any more, plan and act like you'll be here for ten years or more.


One Way to Look at Improving Your Work

Innovation is creative destruction.    When it comes down to doing the work, whether at work, writing, picking stocks, or a school assignment, people tend to want to get done quickly.    This seems obvious, but, creatively destroying your work and doing it again much better is what you want to do.

Blog posts, reports and articles of all sorts usually need several revisions.    At work, we need to practice and maybe even experiment. You aren't going to get stellar results with par or sub-par work.

It takes effort to become much better than average at any craft.    Spend hours, not minutes on a problem when you are the newbie. Take the time to politely drill key points into your protégés.

Everyone has had arm pit bosses and teachers get way to excited and abusive when their rank novice students make mistakes.    Forget them.

When you learn something in your Master Mind, think about, and appreciate as much as you can about what you are learning to do. Look back on the experience, and ask yourself how you can do it better.

In the early days of your MasterMind, teach, and learn skills within your group.    Make your products and communications as good as you can make them.    Be a serious student of your subject, and be impervious to mockers and trolls who want you under their thumb. Take many small actions each day to get closer, and closer to your goal.

My Suggestions for Clearing Blocks

As you probably realize, data mining, encroachment on privacy rights, encroachment on property rights, advertising, and media manipulation are big, HUGE deals.    What you read from pro-government and pro elite news sources will tell you information is big business. As you have heard, we are in the information age.

Look at web 3.0. Look at all the "security"

cameras. Look at the tracking, analysis, and mining of communications, purchases, habits, preferences, opinions, and information that really isn't the business of anyone else.    Big Sis needs her hands in all aspects of life. In 1993, Bill Clinton introduced thought cops (diversity officers) to all colleges. Anyone in the path of the thought cop was called a racist.

You better believe there is a war on for your mind, and wallet.    Although the resistance is growing, we have a long way to go.

Anyway, this data is doubtlessly used to try to:

- Sell you highly flawed investments that will burn you

- Help elect phony politicians

- Convince you to make any type of purchase (especially using debt)

- Divert your attention from the real news

- Make you think nonsense is logical, or even moral

- Influence or manipulate your thinking

and behavior

- Make you complacent

- Find subtle or passive ways to punish, isolate, or abuse you (for independent thinking, aka "thought crimes")

- Make you overconfident

- Make you buy things that hurt you

Sure, absolutely everything isn't overtly controlled or monitored. But it's being worked on.   The focus isn't on your bliss, but on making the richest, and most powerful even more rich and powerful.

So, focus on your bliss, instead of seeking validation, permission, or approval of others, especially through media or technology.   Look for a way to your bliss that works.   Don't seek the cookie cutter instructions and templates for sheeple, if you can help it.   Don't let the sound bites, judgment, entertainment, or fear of crooked authorities stop you from designing a life that is as close to perfect as you can make for yourself.   Don't watch their shows.   Don't purchase their stuff.

Be careful with any type of advisor; especially if your advisor profits in any outcome. Many businesses, and colleges are collecting all sorts of data, "to better help and serve" you. I'm sure no advisor anyplace is trying to sway public opinion or **use** their client's information improperly.

Like I said in the first two volumes of this series, be impervious to negativity. Be sure to allow a little time for fun, comedy, friends, and family, or the other side wins. Be wary of phony friends who knife and mock you. Be wary of their pastors and other "superiors" too. Remember the Tall Poppy Syndrome. As Steve Jobs said, "Don't let the noise of others' opinions drown out your inner voice."

Figure out how you and the members of your MasterMind can turn negative feelings into good work.

Anyway, focus on your bliss. Think about your greatest achievements, short term goals, values, and meaningful life experiences. Make plans that suit your ability. Decide what you can and will sacrifice and work on to reach your next accomplishments or your BHAG. What will you do to get the edge in your life? Take action. Do what you can, today, and every day.

If you are getting bad mouthed by some hypocrite troll, don't get depressed.    Get a good workout in.    Don't overeat or under eat. Your enemies really know psychology, and sociology. Keep this in mind.

No matter what course of action you may decide to take, there are gurus, marketers, and other "leaders" that will mock you, and make false accusations against you.    Get too good at something and gain respect, and some loser will try to bring you down, or steal from you.    Look at how Fred Thompson and Sarah Palin are knifed by "conservative leaders."

Make your to-do list.    Do the simple stuff first. Gain momentum.    Don't do things to make you appear to be busy or whatever.    Keep in mind the emotional benefits you should feel when you're done.    Avoid distractions, if at all possible.    Remind yourself you are keeping your word, etc.

## Separate From the Crowd

How to separate from the crowd? Think laterally.    Question.    Recognize agendas. Look for self-serving rules.    Where does the "new" esoteric wisdom come from?    What cosmic coincidences do you notice?    Don't take bait. Ask what comes next.    Ask yourself if you'll regret doing what the pusher says.

**If you can get answers to your questions and find the real deal, you are valuable to your MasterMind, and no one can call you a sheeple**.    People get paid and volunteer to promote, and celebrate horse shit all the time. Follow the money.    Whose ages old agenda does the paid crowd push on you?    I'm not just talking U.S. politics; I'm talking global enslavement, golden handcuffs at work, diversions from your bliss, taking on too much debt, cheating on your spouse to please the guys at work, and screwing someone for your "superior."

There is a person in my MMG who actually calls the gurus and people he follows for first hand advice, opinion, and whatnot.    He is not afraid of being hung up on or laughed at. Frequently, people like health gurus, sales gurus, and others, give my friend news and ideas before they hit the mainstream (or the alternative stream?).    If you have a great question, send an email to your guru or call him or her.

## Affirmation Tapes for Your Bliss

I can't guarantee these will work every time.    I also won't suggest using affirmations in place of medical care.    But give these affirmations a try.

My commands to myself at this time override all other commands to myself.

My body and mind obey my commands.

Conditions are perfect for _____.

I am certain I can _____    .

My attention is power.

I focus my attention on _____.

I star in the movie where I _____.

_____ is worth doing.

Negative thoughts are replaced by miracles.

Brain unfreeze.

I get the quality of life I expect and demand from myself.

Self-discipline today leads to more options tomorrow.

Chase your dreams and ambitions with all your soul.

I pray like everything depends on God; I work like everything depends on me.

I see opportunities.

I demonstrate remarkable self-control.

You are becoming more and more resourceful.

Then follow these up with an affirmation that states your goal.    Keep your desired outcome somewhat believable and actionable. Cancel out doubts, apathy, and the like as they enter your mind.    Think about the emotional payoffs to getting what you want.

You can record yourself repeating your affirmations. Affirmations tapes can be great for changing your state.    You might want to look into **instant** hypnotic inductions.

Let's change gears here completely.

## Outshine the Master

"Never outshine the master", one bestselling author wrote.    I'd sometimes say to do the opposite.    Keep in mind there is risk.    You will probably look rude and you don't have to brag. But if you can best your master, I'd say let your light shine.    If your master is apathetic or corrupt and you can outperform him at your skill or talent, go for it.

Demonstrate you are better than an ex-boss. Don't just cap off with insults against your ex-boss.    Look at the battling between politicians and between financial gurus.    When a competitor steps on a guru's turf, or one person out does the previous master, there's a good chance of trouble.

If you are stuck, consider building an alternative to the existing product or business.    If you have a problem with an existing product, make a new one.    Look at Open Office, and

Microsoft.    Look at Bitcoin against paper currency.    Look at YouTube against TV news, and seminars versus public colleges.

Listen to Get Abundance, by Dr. Peter Diamandis.    That guy challenged the status quo, and has good stories to tell.


Learn a Little About a Lot

When you are gathering information, be sure to research on your own.    There are plenty of people who want to police your thoughts, take your money, and worse.    Whether we are talking about school, work, or anything, there are schemers, fools, and tyrants.

Don't be afraid to examine content deemed "inappropriate" by your "superiors."    If you are sold on an expert, read the expert's book. Censorship isn't called censorship anymore. Truth is hate speech.

When I was an undergraduate, I was told to read Newsweek, the New York Times, and assigned readings.    Instead, I picked the brains of people I was told were bad.    So, talk to people who retired early, built a business, lived over 100 years, ran political campaigns, and so forth.    But keep in mind, the establishment is pretty jealous.

Becoming an expert at another subject or skill is a good idea.    But my point is to do some reading and ask questions about things that lie ahead in your life.    Trolls are ready to lie, confuse, demean, and slander you. Just get a thumbnail sketch of what you need to know. At least look outside the lines.

Then take action.

When you meet pros, ask them where they think their business, and their industry is headed.    What are the challenges, and opportunities they face?    Ask about trends, and any other vital information you need. Asking questions like these helps you identify where the edge is.    You may want to go to the edge, and gamble on stocks. Or, do market research for new products to sell.    You could try to determine if your course needs to be adjusted.

Put This Law to Work for You...

...the law of accumulation. Success in pretty near anything is a result of countless small actions that add up over time. Don't let your treadmill or weights accumulate dust. Accumulate short workouts in spare time. You'll look and feel better.

Take extra money and buy a little physical silver when you can. Cut little expenses, and contribute to your regular, non-IRA account. Read and talk to people in your field often and become as knowledgeable as you can.

Your cash will slowly pile up. You'll be a more confident person as a result of honestly making, and saving money. AND, you can afford and qualify for more and better deals the more money and experience you have.


Problems to Overcome

As I said in the first volume of this series, "There is peer pressure to put on the dunce cap." Don't submit yourself to anyone who wants you to put on the dunce cap. People who just go with the flow, like a dead fish, or do what the bullies want are just sheeple.    You'll get no energy from them.

Don't collaborate with go nowhere types. Avoid go nowhere types.    Go nowhere types are your most heinous foes. They lack confidence, lack resolve, need approval, are glued to Monday morning quarterbacks, nit-pick, have petty power trips, and are misleading.

Go nowhere types waste time, suck energy, are unstable, and will turn a good workplace or any organization into a concentration camp.    They will bait you and then burn you.    They will pose as rock ribbed conservatives and then reveal they are total liars who want something for nothing, and they will slander you.

Associate with people who are genuine. Connect with people who lead themselves, not with those who go with the flow.    If you want, you can just float downstream and find out where are the dead fish are.


David vs. Goliath

Read success stories from time to time.    As I'm sure you are reminded all the time, the odds against success are pretty long. What I am suggesting is to read about people who overcame long odds.     As Kiyosaki told us, David used leverage (a slingshot) against Goliath.

A slingshot was David's weapon. What weapons do you have at your disposal to help your business or career?     To get your web site to critical mass, you need to tailor your message on your site to your target audience.     It needs to be clear to your reader what they should do. Using the right keywords and SEO is important. You also need inbound links from sites with tons of traffic, not just Google.     You need your customers to advertise for you for free.

Your site probably has tons of competition. So, again, have a target customer.     Write quality blog posts and ezine articles, and op-ed's in a newspaper to get traffic.     Get a couple people with bigger audiences to repost your articles.

Look for competitive advantages.     Be prepared for questions.     Attempt to overcome any possible criticisms of you, your products, and your sites.     Don't treat a troll like the Mayor, or some VIP.     Trolls just want to look important and waste your time.

Here's another success story, Finland against Russia in 1939.    In 1939, Russia sent over a million troops to invade Finland.    Russia used tanks and airplanes.    Finland used their knowledge of their terrain and improvised weapons to beat the Russians.

These days, entrepreneurs use technology to defeat their competitors.    The first companies to the Internet, web 2.0, and web 3.0 were frequently big winners when companies used these technologies correctly.    From time to time, look at business web sites and magazines that will tell you about new technologies, products, and strategies that could help you, or that you could invest in.    I have a list of great news sites at http://www.renegadeuniversity.net    on the Links page.

Andrew Carnegie has a good success story. Carnegie had humble origins.    But, he was a hard worker.    Carnegie also saved and entered the steel business when it was somewhat new. He didn't sit back and watch TV and procrastinate.    He did seek advice from and start a Master Mind group.    Tony Robbins advises **stretching**.    That is what Carnegie did, stretch.    There were no guarantees of success for Carnegie.

Jeff Bezos quit a Wall Street brokerage in 1994 and launched Amazon dot com. Before long, Bezos allowed third party sellers to sell used books and CDs on Amazon for a fee.    That's pretty close to passive income right there. Bezos became a billionaire when Amazon became profitable in 2002.

Closer to home, a young lawyer named Gordon Smith inherited a pea farm in eastern Oregon. Gordon turned the farm completely around, and made millions. Smith ran for public office, quickly becoming Oregon's Majority Leader. Gordon Smith later was elected to the U.S. Senate.

Anthony Robbins grew up sh*t broke.    But Robbins loved learning and finding solutions to help people he went to school with.    Robbins succeeded as a salesman, only to become broke again, living in a tiny apartment. One year later, Anthony Robbins lived in a castle after creating success with Robbins Research Institute and his seminar business.

The co-founder of my Master Mind group is one of the most ardent disciples of Tony Robbins I have ever heard of. CANI (constant and never ending improvement) is a part of his daily routine and thought process. After knowing Bob, our co-founder, and member for over 10 years, I can see his has reached goals in every area of life. We still have no island, but we're not knifing coworkers for some chocolates from bosses at crappy jobs or begging for scraps from Lucifer's table.

Richard Branson had trouble in school. But that didn't stop him from starting Virgin Records and a plethora of other businesses. Branson's mother would not allow him to become a wimp, as Dr. Gene Landrum points out as a determinant of Branson's success.

Brian Tracy grew up in poverty and did not graduate from high school. Brian Tracy worked at various laboring jobs until he became a salesman. Tracy learned from the best salesmen at his company until he was promoted into management. Since then, Brian Tracy has managed and turned around several companies and has written best-selling books.

Discuss success stories in your MMG from time to time.    Find examples of what you are trying to achieve at Inc, Forbes, Fast Company, and other sites.    Be wary of trolls who will bait and switch you, mock achievement, worship leftist heroes, etc.

One Person Can Make All the Difference

Think about people in your life or that you read about that made all the difference to you, or the population of the world, or to people you care about.    By reading positive materials, and documentaries on YouTube, you hopefully feel inspired. As you have doubtlessly noticed, otherwise average people have changed the course of history and improved the lives of many people.    What positive attributes did your favorites have? Rosa Parks wasn't a lawyer.    She was just courageous.    Anyone could be courageous.

Let's look at a list of what kinds of people could make all the difference, especially for a MMG.

-    The will to sacrifice and to do what others won't.

- A mentor.

- An advocate.

- A determined and diligent worker.

- An inventor.

- The diligent campaign staffer.

- The person who puts fear aside and stands up to a bully.

- The web site designer who works tirelessly to make sure the target customer has the best experience possible at his client's site.

- The manager who works alongside the grunts to keep tabs on their experience and the customer's experience.

There are potentially many others, but this is a good start.    Being able to say, "We need to have X's attitude, or do what Y did" is a plus.

## The Opt-In List

5000 friends on Facebook can be awesome.    A forum with 100,000 members would be awesome.    A large opt-in list is equally as good.

As you know, you can sell to your list and get them to do what you want.    The big problem is getting people to sign up.    One solution is quality freebies.    Another solution is your product is in demand and people want to get it first.

But anyway, a special report, a free audio, video, or eBook should lure some subscribers. Your freebies cannot be sales pitches or people will unsubscribe.    Your freebie must be quality. It must solve a problem or be entertaining.

Joint ventures can build your list.    Find a marketer in your field and interview him or her, or have the other interview you.    The audio could be a great lure for subscribers for both of you.    If your product is on Clickbank, your JV partner is sure to get paid.    Otherwise, you have to determine how many sales your JV partner is responsible for and cut him a check (or PayPal).

**You are not above building your list person by person**.

You don't have to type up long newsletters or write every day.    Simply send information to your subscribers that they want.

You can put affiliate ads in your emails.    You can work affiliate text links in your article. Don't expect to live off of an affiliate income. Really good emails to your subscribers may get forwarded to others.    As you can see, that's free advertising.

Find some lists you have subscribed to.    See if one of those sites can be used as a template for your sales letter.    At my opt-in page, I say "Get a sneak preview of Black Book of the Master Mind 1 and 2."    When the site visitor signs up, they get the eBook.    Plus, the prospect sees an ad for Subliminal Power.    I hardly ever send emails to my list.

Your list can and should provide targeted traffic to your sites or a site you want them to look at.

A site you should look at, use, and study is Iwillteachyoutoberich dot com.    Ramit Sethi offers help starting side hustles in exchange for your email address.    You may want to model Sethi's site.

Start building a list today; even you aren't sure exactly how you will use it in the next few days or months.


A Semi Passive Income

Although most major consumer needs are met through the Internet, you can still generate a semi passive income from the web.    What you want to do is match buyers with sellers (EBay, Amazon, and many specialized site do this). Or sell a subscription based product (newsletters, forums, the use of software, etc.)    And then you have renting or leasing of equipment.

There are real estate and paper investments, too.    But a lot is written about them elsewhere.    I have a page at www.renegadeuniversity.net about paper passive income investments.    Right now, I like an ETF with the ticker PSP.    PSP currently pays dividends of over 1% a month.

Borrowing funds at one of the lowest rates on earth and investing for one of the highest returns on earth is an idea to consider.    Look outside your country for opportunities, and yields.


MasterMind Facts and Ideas that Work

- Keep in mind that "social skills" help fool people into accepting tyranny, and common scams.    I first noticed this in the early 1990's.    "What if they had absolute power and made decisions for you, but they were nice and caring?' No way, it's still tyranny.    You'd have to marry into royal blood to really make it big."

- "This isn't an official _____ activity." Enough suckers are born, bred, and brainwashed into believing or allowing illegal or unethical activities are actually not a part of the company, or other organization's policy.

- Ask your foe's straw man what will become of him after his boss gets done with him. Unemployment? Back to school? An honorable job?    Look at

the Georgia Guidestones sometime.
Try to determine the need for the straw
man to exist after the decision is made
to eliminate 80% of the world's
population.

- Make the other side obsolete.   Bush
  made the GOP obsolete by distancing
  himself from conservatives, watering
  down legislation to gain two democrat
  votes, giving away the store, and not
  siding with Constitutionalists
  consistently.   Obama made McCain
  obsolete by making expensive promises
  the government can only afford for so
  long.

- Make products which make other
  products obsolete, even yours.
  Protect your IP and build a solid
  business. Your need your MasterMInd
  to have the knowledge and skills that
  help you.

- Kiyosaki says your word is an asset.   If
  you can get a signature loan, a date, a
  decent job, if people generally accept
  your word, or a favor of a sensitive
  nature, your word is an asset.

-   Too much TV and videos **can** leave you a rat in a cage.    If Fox news, CNBC, or motivational YouTube videos take time away from reaching your dreams, then cut back. Follow the money and the affiliations.

-   While building your networks, and lists, be sure to weed out detractors and any type of troll.    These trolls want to truncate your message, smear you, and they are very jealous of your success. What's that about social skills, and ethics?

-   Remember, your fate largely depends on you.    Your boss probably won't make you rich or even comfortable. Too many church people are fat and lazy and are ready to lambaste people with "prosperity doctrines."    Too many young adults wait for teacher to give permission. Replace horseshit with the affirmation, "If it's to be it's up to me."

-   Your confidence and self-esteem will rise as you knock out goals and objectives. If you don't feel your accomplishments are important at all, this does not mean you should have low self-esteem.    You don't have to become big headed, or arrogant. Nope, you'll help people learn, earn, and grow.    Forget the critics who preach socialism, apathy, and death to billions of sheeple.    Foes will try to take credit for your accomplishments, steal from you, and/or slander you.

- When I was a kid, I went to a youth group meeting where a "leader" brought in a buddy or two and started in with, "Bringing ya down bro! You can't hope to succeed.    Don't even try!"    I'm sorry, but I am not sold on many churches here on the west coast. There are way too many similarities between churches, progressive organizations, public schools, and a couple other organizations.    If some well-credentialed troll screams you're a heretic, you might treat that like a badge of honor.    But brush up on your knowledge of the Bible just in case.

- When some well-credentialed crook tries to put the sh*t back in the horse, don't go along. Maybe cause a commotion. Tell your side what you observed. Persist until you're sure both sides aren't the same. Trolls here on the west coast don't like to acknowledge, even though they are blessed with social skills (farted on them by unicorns).

- Before the 1990's churches used to advocate private schools, and homeschooling. Now many churches are connected at the pelvis with public schools.

- There is a difference between poverty and a lack of ambition.

- Don't let circumstances or external forces define or dictate anything in regards to you, your self-worth, self-esteem, etc.

- When I was a kid, my classmates and I were taught being a type A was bad and serving a type A was the best career move. B.S. man, be a type A.

- Stop unnecessary "work", worry, fear, entertainment, indecision, pleasing abusive people, scheming, and mental masturbation.    Work on your dreams instead.    Don't allow excuses.    If for some strange reason you can't, then meditate, and pray.    If funds are limited, do what you can.    Take a look at my site if you need funds or motivation.

- Words about strategy, and warfare that our friends, and servants can't hear us say: smokescreens, bait and switch, smearing, straw men, delay game, ambush, fraud, hoodwinker, misquote, accident, framing, Stockholm Syndrome, bribery, apathy, social skills, unofficial, and I could go on.

Conquering Overwhelm

If you have a 32 item list of to-do's, should do, and attainable goals you can accomplish, just get started with taking one item and doing it. Don't allow excuses.    Do everything you can before the deadline or before bed.

Push through the discomfort involved in getting your stuff done.    You'll feel great afterwards. And you'll have the payoff each item on your list offers.    You will feel better when you're done with your tasks.

Another idea would be to cluster tasks.    Group some of your objectives and take them out one by one.

Just knock out item after item on your to-do list. Don't take the time to do motivational hypnosis or affirmations unless you are certain nothing will get done if you don't. A quick rest break will help if you need it.

Deal with customer service reps; replace software or passwords, etc. Don't let little hassles stop you.    If you need motivation, watch the videos pages at my site(s).

After you've made a good deal of progress, call someone from your MMG or post to your list or forum.    If you discovered things by annihilating your to-do list and are on a tear, your MMG will benefit too.

Anyway, this is common sense, but you have to understand, your Master Mind must push each other out of your comfort zones, through blocks, and to personal freedom.

Look Beyond Constraints

Look past any and all constraints, bottlenecks, limiting beliefs, and so forth.    Question anything pertinent to yourself, your MMG, your retirement, and your business.    Question your rules, feelings, and beliefs.    List all the things that have gotten in your way in your past. Then write down your solutions and resolve that the old excuses are no longer acceptable.

Be creative and truthful as you plan how to overcome your obstacles.    Spin off of impossible ideas that you may have when you brainstorm.    Take action right away.    Don't be deterred by hassles, uncomfortable conversations, and hard work.    Get your MasterMind to help if you need it.

Remember Anthony Robbins affirmation, "God and I are One and God is everything."    To help overcome any obstacles, imagine that everything is one.    Don't expect miracles from this, but I have found it useful to imagine everything as one, because it forces us to change our approach to problems.

Jim Cramer is fond of saying "there's always a bull market somewhere."   In my experience, this is largely true.   You have to find that bull market.   When you do, your optimism will soar and if you use the inspiration, you can get loads more work done.

Earl Nightengale says our minds are like soil. You can plant whatever you want, the soil doesn't care.   So decide to plant an abundance of good things and have the courage to stick to it when the going gets tough.

Your destiny depends on your actions.   Don't depend on the government, party leaders, Wall Street, or churches to live up to their promises or to look out for your best interests.   The scandal is what's legal.   The prescription for the masses is to follow orders, take your fluoride, watch TV all day, and repeat stupid shit from tools that allegedly have superior people skills.

Again, have the courage to stick to your goals and ideals.   Fear and panic don't help at all. Acts of courage can turn the tide in your favor right away.    As Robert Kiyosaki's rich dad said, "prepare for bad times and you'll only know good times."    If sheeple and uber sheeple around you disagree, or become enraged, you have to know you're on to something.

Don't Be Afraid of Being Called an Extremist

Most famous people in history can be called "extremists."    Most really successful people "go all out" or are unreasonable when it comes to their goals and passions.    Are "gazelle intense" Dave Ramsey listeners extreme?    Yes. Are professional athletes extreme?    Of course, they have to be.

Don't worry about unconstructive criticism. Don't fret if some dunce calls your passions or goals "your God."    Avoid trolls.    Don't waste a lot of time getting trolls to cooperate.    There are institutions that train, and encourage trolls.

**Prove your detractors wrong**.    That should be motivation.    Don't be afraid to go against what the schools and media or anyone prescribe for the masses.    You aren't the masses.    Follow your bliss and be unreasonable.    Be ready to bounce back from failure and defeat. Accept full responsibility for your life. Accepting responsibility gives you control.

Tell your MasterMind group to **own** their day, their lives, and their emotions. Ask yourself tough questions. Make real decisions. What if you fail? People survive failure, and different "nightmares" all the time, come on.


Work On Your Dreams

Again, don't sit and watch movies you've already seen after work. Avoid wasting time, or money. Work on your own projects.

If you encounter writer's block, or any other block, imagine calling a member of your MasterMind. Explain the block you are experiencing. If you know your MasterMind, you could anticipate what they'd say to help you. Describing your block or dilemma is helpful. Being clear about what you do want gives you more clarity. It's much easier to have well defined goals.

Asking or visualizing asking for help can get you through a block.    Bring solutions to your MMG that they may find helpful.


Beware of Trolls

I have found that some people really like to play games.    It is good to have an emergency fund in case you find yourself swamped by trolls who want to intimidate you, bait you, or rip you off. It might be best to cut and run.

Unfortunately, many well-credentialed crooks are looking for windfalls from valueless schemes.    You have to protect yourself, and your assets from them.    Crooks are no fun at work either.    I have encountered many coworkers, and managers that didn't really understand things like integrity, respecting the will of the client, wasting company resources, and so forth.

Many companies are connected with poor political and social movements at the pelvis. This isn't always for the good of the parties involved.    If they were crooks when you are little, they are crooks now. Keep your powder dry.    Be wary of trolls.

Schools, in general, fail to teach common sense topics like The Bill of Rights, basic business, legal, and economics information.    The schools push for global governance.    Using scams is an everyday practice.    High schools used to show a film that said the world would run out of gas by the year 2000.    Do you know who is pushing Common Core?    Being independent these days is getting tougher, and lonelier. Prepare for challenges as best you can.    You'll find a MasterMind essential.    Keep parasites at bay.

Again, people who convert parasites, and warn their neighbors against trolls are mocked by "society."    Who funds the trolls?    Huge money.    Alex Jones, Michael Savage, and Rush Limbaugh really aren't so bad. People who think they'll personally profit from the dog and pony show, or, a military police state, and a vast bureaucracy don't agree.

Anyone can drink the communist kool-aid and still get burned.    Remember, on the flip side, John the Baptist was executed for telling the truth.

The elites are battling each other for control. The government can't afford to give the elites contracts, and pet projects anymore.    Future bail outs will need to be kept real quiet.    The government, in lieu of cash, makes unnecessary laws, and bash the individuals, and even races the elites want bashed.

Keep in mind, the elites wanted to bring the U.S. down to the level of the rest of world for years.    "Mainstream" republicans said little. Conspiracies are beeeyad.    "We don't talk like those people" was something I used to hear when I was younger, when someone suggested the two party system was a scam.

So Now What?

I dumped a lot of negative information on you. Now it's time to look for solutions.    Like I said, look for ways to turn negative feelings into good, focused work. Form a MasterMind. Face fears.    Keep it closed.

Look at conspiracy theories, and the news, and question what you are told.    Let me give you a plausible example. Some people fear mass exterminations of people for population control.   But, why would billionaires want to invest in farm land, now, if people were going to be wiped out soon?   Why would stock pickers talk about buying shares of luxury brands, if people are going to be sacrificed to the earth, rather than join the middle class?

Look for solutions. Investment gurus have kept the winds of major trends, and government demands, at their backs.   Get together with your MMG. Follow the money.   Search for opportunity. Read any of the following you need to until you've found your opportunity:

- 10K and 10Q statements

- Industry magazines

- Academic journals

- Corporate web sites

- Government and quasi government web sites

- Blogs from authorities in your niche

- Call the person who may have the answer to your question

- Quality investing newsletters

- Forbes

- Local newspapers & web sites

Be aware there could be a problem with any source you may find. The search results of search engines are skewed. You can use Google Alerts for up to date information.

Stand Firm

There is a saying in Oregon that goes, "when the leader is struck the sheeple scatter." Read into what I'm saying there. If you don't think the saying is right, look at recent GOP history.

It takes courage to stand firm. Stand firm for yourself, your MasterMInd, and anything you see fit. Why sell yourself out for some all things to all people man child of the stratosphere? Why worry about the criticism and judgment from total hypocrites?

Like I have said, there is pressure to put on the dunce cap. It's a temptation to be lazy and sloppy.    Poor leaders will try to get you lower yourself to the level of a rat for a pittance.

Believe in yourself.    Have the courage to advance your dreams and causes every single day.    Be responsible for your life, and the responsibilities you can control.


Investing in a Nutshell

Start a portfolio at Yahoo or Seeking Alpha. Add stocks you want to follow in your portfolio. Take the time to find out if dividends have increased for the last several years.    Increasing dividends is usually a good sign. Be sure to look at the stock's 52 week high and low, too.

Read the last three 10K and 10Q reports for your companies.    This will give you a thumbnail view of strengths, weaknesses, opportunities, and threats (SWOT).    10K and 10Q reports offer guidance to you the investor from the company's management.    You can look at items like free cash flow, and the company's expenses in the reports. Sometimes companies lie in their reports. Most people would avoid buying shares of a company that lie to prospective and current shareholders.

Insider buying, and increasing returns on investment are two things to look at, too. There is no fool proof formula.    But these factors can help you find winners.    Another obvious thing is to buy, considering the above, in the midst of a recession.

There may be a problem waiting for a recession. The current administration wants to flatten out the economic cycle to prevent booms, and busts. I wouldn't venture a guess as to how this attempt will pan out.    This may mean to search for otherwise solid companies that are temporarily down.    This also pushes investors into maybe buying shares of companies that aren't profitable yet. Buying unprofitable companies is very risky.

Another thing is to be wary of advertisers, and newsletters that push extreme fear or are way too optimistic.    You want to buy quality shares when the masses are full of fear, and sell when the dumb money gets thrown around.

I see ads selling newsletters, and reports that talk about new technologies, and other developments.    You can try a couple of those newsletters if you want.    But knowing as much as you can find out about your sectors, and subsectors for free can save you a lot of cash. When you hear talk of some change or revolution, try to determine what the change means to you, and the pocketbooks of companies.

Entrepreneurship

How quickly could you actually launch a business?    If you have no idea how to start a business, you should learn how.    Even if you don't intend to start a new venture, you may need to understand entrepreneurship.    Your boss and prospective employers might wish you understood vital details like:

- Feasibility studies

- Market research

- Budgeting, seed money, and angel investors

- Branding and advertising

- Taxes (domestic and foreign)

- Knowing and understanding customers and target customers

- P.R., damage control, social media, press releases, appropriate web site design for corporate site.

- Doing business overseas

- Product design

- Preventing corporate espionage

What I was getting at is when you have your idea before you hit the hay, would you have any clue how to form an LLC, buy a domain, set up a site, protect your IP, get your customers, etc.? Read Launching New Ventures, by Kathleen R Allen.

Learn From the Hustlas

Occasionally, when I was in school, I'd give the answer and the teacher would say "wrong." Like when a hustla teacher had me show where Jordan was on the map.    I pointed straight to Jordan on the map and she says that's not it.

I've had many experiences like that with employers and potential employers too.

The point is to know you are right, and you're not so right the Children of the Stratosphere should actually be offended.    It's odd because the hustlas, who are never manipulative, bossy, or opinionated, are just helping us not be so serious, studious, and "one dimensional." When you attempt to dare some better thing, in a rigged contest, expect Salinsky like tactics from your bankrupt "superiors."


Who's Kissing Your Ass?

On a device people spend too much time with called the TV, actors playing dopes on the street accept interviews with reporters, and hilarity ensues.    I understand this is just entertainment, but it gives the viewer a false sense of confidence.    Plenty of people who claim to represent Fox news viewers seem to accidentally screw up, delay important work, and lose to the other side.    All while soaking up lobbying money, bribes, and so forth.    To think people keep the dog and pony show going for free, or even for punishment.

There Is No Insulation from Life, At Least Not For You

You've heard of corporate welfare.    I'm sure you're aware public employees want absolutely every benefit to mitigate every trial, and risk we all face in life (except military veterans).

You and I don't get the same benefits.    We have to fend for ourselves.    We have to worry about what the government, the Federal Reserve, the U.N., Bilderberg, and Tammany Hall want to do to us.    How many people would you say are concerned with choosing whether to bow down, flee, or fight those people?

Try to organize resistance, and see what happens, even if it's just an experiment.    Try to insulate yourself from crime, privacy threats, and avoid any aspect of Big Sis you want, and see what happens.

## Leave Problems at Low Levels

Years ago, I had a capable supervisor who told his team, it's better to leave problems where they are, and handle them yourself, rather than cry to upper management.   On the other hand, if things are going too smoothly, you might have upper management giving you problems to deal with.   If the boss won't be promoted, why would you?   Therefore you can't that great.   Squeaky wheels get replaced.

## Health is Wealth

Acidity is bad.   An alkaline body is good.   Real food, which means all fresh, preferably organic fruit, vegetables, and nuts are what you want to eat.   Juicing fruit and vegetables is awesome for you. It is very tough for cancer to survive in an alkaline environment.

Like I said, acidity is bad.   Coffee is acidic. Black coffee prevents diabetes.   But coffee is acidic.   Stress is acidic.   Like I said, figure out how to turn fear into awesome work.   This may help.   Relaxation, meditation, exercise, and laughter are good relievers of stress.

I have a friend who said headaches are caused by the way you think. Since he told me that, I've had very few headaches. Bob used to tell me about the six human needs. I will put a video about the 6 human needs on my site.

Be ready with jokes, one-liners, quips, pick-up lines, and any non-acidic verbiage you feel you could use when you're out and about. Committing some jokes to memory and straining your brain for a good list of handy ice breakers should make you feel good.

Get to Work Pal

The world is your oyster. Own your thoughts, feelings, and actions. Be responsible with everything under your control. Make decisions wisely. Lead your MasterMind by example. Keep your game on the ground. Common sense may not always be exciting, but we must have it. Stick to your principles or you'll just be a wandering sheeple. Accept the challenge.

And remember, doing evil will not produce good.

For Further Reading:

Learn Any Foreign Language, Dagny Taggart

The Obstacle is the Way, Ryan Holiday

Emergency, Neill Strauss

Doing the Impossible, Patrick Bet-David

The Strangest Secret, Earl Nightengale

The Little Book of Big Profits From Small Stocks, Hillary Kramer

Innovation and Entrepreneurship, Peter Drucker

Launching New Ventures, Kathleen R Allen

The Sovereign Individual, James D Davidson and William Rees-Mogg

# Wachsen Algen für Profit:

## Wie man einen Photobioreaktor für Wachsende Algen für Proteine bauen, Lipide, Kohlenhydrate, Anti-Oxidantien, Biokraftstoffe, Biodiesel und andere Wertvolle Metaboliten

## von Christopher Kinkaid

Solardyne.com

Published by Solardyne, LLC
Portland, Oregon

ISBN-13: 978-1500582180
ISBN-10: 1500582182

# Inhaltsverzeichnis

# Vorwort

Algen ist ein Wunder der Natur. Rich, in Aminosäuren, Proteine, Lipide, Kohlenhydrate, Anti-Oxidantien, Phycobiliproteinen und andere wertvolle Produkte, Algen wird als neuer Rohstoff über die Branchen erschlossen.

Dieses Book beschreibt, wie Sie Ihre eigenen Photobioreaktor zu bauen, um reinen Algenarten (Taxa) wachsen.

Algen sind Earths "Motor," um das Nahrungsnetz zu tanken. Als "Primärproduzent," fast die Hälfte der Sauerstoffproduktion auf der Erde verantwortlich ist, ist die Kraft der Algen kommerzialisiert, wertvolle Bio-Produkte zu produzieren. Bauen Sie Ihre eigene, Algen Photobioreaktor (PBR) wachsen-Kit, um wertvolle Algenstämme kultivieren, und tippen Sie in der schnell wachsenden Algen-Industrie.

Algen wachsen Zuverlässigkeit, und wiederholt, mit Photobioreaktor (PBR) Algen wachsen Kits für kontrollierte Photosynthese. Wachsen bis zu vier verschiedene Algen Taxa mit diesen 4-Gefäß-Algen wachsen Kits bewertet bei 80 Liter Gesamtkapazität.

Komplett mit optischen, mechanischen, elektrischen, pneumatischen und biologischen Systemen, Photobioreaktoren geben Ihnen die vollständige Kontrolle. Wachsende Monokulturen von Algen, mit Photobioreaktoren, ist für Forscher, Entwickler, Unternehmen, Universitäten, und denen, die Algen Monokulturen mit Reinheit kultivieren müssen, und minimale Kosten für den Bau.

Algen, produzieren wertvolle Aminosäuren, Proteine, Kohlenhydrate und essentielle Öle (Lipide) verbrauchen Wasser-borne Belastung für Nährstoffe. Algen-Arten, mit PBR Algen gewachsen wachsen Kits ermöglichen es Forschern, enorme Produktivität Algen in der Lage, in der Masse in 24 Stunden unter exponentiellen Wachstumsphase verdoppeln erschließen. Algenforscher, zu arbeiten, um Protokolle für die Steigerung der Produktion zu entwickeln.

Wachsende Algen wandelt Wasser in organische Verbindungen (CO2), und die Sonnenstrahlung in wertvoller organischer Moleküle. Dieses Book ist als Ressource für den Aufbau Ihrer eigenen Photobioreaktor und wachsende wertvollen Algenstämme geschrieben.

Dieses Book geschrieben wird, als Ressource für Forscher, um eine effektive Bioreaktor, bewertet bei 80 Liter, für den Anbau von Algen Monokulturen zu konstruieren. Isoliert von Verschmutzung, diese Photobioreaktoren, bieten dem Forscher die totale Kontrolle über alle Ein-und thermodynamischen Bedingungen, um eine bestimmte Monokultur Algenstamm wachsen.

Wachsen Algen für Profit mit Photobioreaktoren, um nützliche Mengen reinen Arten (Taxa) zu produzieren. Wachsen Algen Biomasse, für Ihre Experimente oder zu verkaufen, mit diesem einfach zu Build Photobioreaktor.

# Über das Buch

Dieses Book geschrieben wird, als Ressource für den Aufbau Ihrer eigenen Photobioreaktor (PBR), für Algenwachstum und Anbau.

Ihre Photobioreaktor mit Laborgeräte in einem Bierbrau-Shop leicht zugänglich, und anderen Herstellern gebaut werden. Verwenden Glasgefäße, ungiftig Schläuche, Weiden Kurven und andere wesentliche Elemente, in den örtlichen Baumärkten, um Ihre PBR bauen.

**Ein Kapitel** befasst sich mit dem großen Bild von wachsenden Algen. Aquatische Arten haben besondere Anforderungen. Algen, sind sehr robust, dennoch, sehr zart in ihrer bevorzugten Bedingungen. Die Algen können Grubber Photobioreaktoren (PBR) zu verwenden, um die wachsende Umgebung zu kontrollieren.

**Kapitel Zwei** unterschiedliche Bewertungen Algenarten von Interesse und Potential, und wesentlichen Wert Branchen, von der Kosmetik, Fisch, und Tierfutter, um Nutraceuticals, Antioxidationsmittel, und Biokraftstoffe. Includes, Artenliste, für Ihre Aufmerksamkeit.

**Kapitel Drei** beschreibt Ihre Photobioreaktor (PBR) Hardware-und Stücklisten. Die PBR enthält Beleuchtungselemente, mechanischen Rahmen, eine Luftpumpe und Filtersystem, mit Weide der

Kurven, um eine Kontamination zu stoppen. Die PBR Kit verwendet Glas und 100% ungiftig Food Grade Kunststoffschlauch zum Einleiten von Luft in die Wachstumsgefäßen.

**Vier Kapitel** umfasst Algen Optik. Als ein "Photo-Bioreaktor", Algen benötigen spezifische "optisch" Bedingungen für ein optimales Wachstum. Kapitel vier werden die verschiedenen "Trigger" und Anforderungen, die Algenwachstumsraten, und Produkte aus einer optischen Perspektive zu stimulieren.

**Fünf Kapitel** beschreibt die Ernährungsanforderungen von Algen. Als aquatische Arten, Algen und Kieselalgen, sind sehr empfindlich gegen gelösten Elemente in das Wasser, oder das Fehlen von ihnen. Algenwachstum Protokolle, damit die Forscher, um einen bestimmten "Wachstumsprofil" zu bauen, um eine ausgewählte Arten (Taxa) zu kultivieren, und die Kontrolle der von den Algen produzierten Metabolite.

**Sechs Kapitel** befasst sich mit Algen für Biokraftstoffe Einsatzmaterials. Öl sammeln Algen sind sehr erwünscht. Beeinflussung des Wachstumszyklus der Algen für Biokraftstoffe, Biodiesel oder Rohstoff, den Forschern ermöglichen, Protokolle, die Lipidproduktion maximieren.

**Sieben Kapitel** untersucht grundlegende Kulturtechniken zur Messung von Wachstumsraten und Net Algenbiomasseproduktion. Algen, in der Wachstumsphase durch 5 wesentliche Phasen. Akklimatisierung, Compensation Point, exponentiellen Wachstumsphase, Sättigung Point und Schließen Phase. Bearbeiten von Algen, an jedem Punkt in ihrer klassischen Wachstumskurve, geben die Forscher die Fähigkeit, "Trigger" Reaktionen für eine gewünschte Ausgabe.

**Kapitel Acht** sieht Häufig gestellte Fragen über Photobioreaktoren, Bau und Betrieb. Bewertung, Verfahren zum Mischen, Probenahme, Mess, und wachsende Algenkulturen.

**Kapitel Neun** ist eine Kurzanleitung, um Ihre Photobioreaktor Konstruktion. Schritt für Schritt Montage Ihrer mechanischen Rahmen, Wachstum Schiffe, Luftpumpe, Filter-und Beleuchtungssysteme.

# Über den Autor

Christopher Kinkaid

**Christopher (Toby) Kinkaid**, die ursprünglich aus Portland, Oregon ist der Gründer der **Solardyne.com**, **SolarQuote.com** und **AlgaeToday.com** und hat in saubere Energietechnologie seit über drei Jahrzehnten gearbeitet.

Kinkaid, ist der Erfinder des "Helyx," Vertical Axis Wind-Generator, der "Mariposa" Non-Imaging-Solar-Konzentrator PV-Modul (Dauerbetrieb an den Sandia National Laboratory seit 1994), die Solar-Demultiplexer optische Solar konzentrieren Linse (Dr. James / Sandia National Laboratory 1991) und der Erfinder des Original-"Solar Power Pack" (Mutter Erde Nachrichten, "Littlest Utility" Juni / Juli, 2001). Kinkaid hat eine offizielle Dozent und Moderator auf saubere Energietechnologie auf der ganzen Welt, darunter APEC, Bangkok, Thailand, 2003, "Energy Solutions World", Tokyo, Japan, 2003, der internationalen Biomasse-Konferenz (IBC), 2010,

Minneapolis, MN und der Algenbiomasse Organization (ABO)-Konferenz, 2010, Phoenix, AZ.

Kinkaid, hat in Interviews auf KOIN TV, KGW-TV und "Nachhaltige Today" in Oregon hergestellt erschien. Kinkaid hat auf dem Board of Directors für die National Hydrogen Association serviert, in Washington DC, 1993, und die Japan Satellite Communications Company (JCNET), Fukuoka, Japan, 1994-1995.

Kinkaid, serviert auf der Board of Directors für Algaedyne Corporation, Preston, MN, 2010-2013. Kinkaid, dient derzeit als CEO von Solardyne, LLC in Portland, Oregon.

Christopher Kinkaid ist an der Westküste auf der Basis, und seine Arbeit in Solar, Wind, Biomasse und Anwendungen, Forschung und Entwicklung in Portland, Oregon geht weiter.

# Einführung

Algen ist eine Kraft der Natur. Alles Leben auf der Erde geht auf Einzelzellorganismen. Algen sind die Grundlage der aquatischen Nahrungsnetz, und "Motoren" von Sauerstoff, und die Basisernährung Produktivität für unseren Planeten. Halb Sauerstoff auf der Erde kommt von Algen Mikroorganismen. Das intensive Interesse der Industrie in "Algen", wird durch unglaubliche Wachstumsraten, zur Umwandlung von anorganischen Chemikalien, in einige der wertvollsten organische Moleküle auf der Erde angetrieben.

Dieses Book wird geschrieben, um zu beschreiben, wie man ein Photobioreaktor (PBR), für den Anbau von Algen und Kieselalgen bauen. Der Photobioreaktor (PBR), in diesem Book beschrieben, ist entworfen und von Glas Schiffe gebaut, und andere Geräte, leicht zugänglich von Baumärkten, Bierbrauerei, und Labor-Versorgungsunternehmen. Dieses Book enthält ein komplettes Ersatzteilliste für den Bau Ihrer eigenen Photobioreaktoren.

Der Photobioreaktor (PBR) ermöglicht es den Forschern, um alle Algen Taxonomische Divisionen wachsen:

Baciariophyta, Chrlorarchiniophyta, Chlorophyta, Cryptophyta, Cyanophyta, Dinophyta, Euglenophyta, Glaucophytoa, Haptophyta, Herokontophyta und Rhodophyta.

Wachsende Algen ist die ultimative "Golidlocks"-Syndrom. Algen, wie es "genau richtig."

PH-Wert, Temperatur, gelöste CO2, O2, gelöst, Makro-und Mikronährstoffe, bestimmte Metallionen, Vitamine und einem photosynthetisch aktiven Strahlung (PAR) Lichtquelle: Wasserarten Wachstumsraten werden von einem bestimmten (im Bereich von) Bedingungen, einschließlich angetrieben .

Ein Photobioreaktor ist eine kontrollierte Umgebung, die Sie erstellen, um den "sweet spot" der wachsenden Algen, durch die Kontrolle und Manipulation, diese Bedingungen zu schaffen.

Die hier beschriebene PBR wird auf Glas Schiffe, ungiftig Lebensmittelqualität Schläuche, Weiden Biegung, jede Erreger Eingabe Ihrer Gefäße, Druckluftpumpen und 5 Mikrometer-Filter, der Verunreinigungen in der Zuluft zu entfernen behindern basiert.

Dieses Book beschreibt, den Photobioreaktor-Hardware, die Sie für Ihr Labor aufbauen können, sowie Diskussionen über Nährstoffe, Licht, Sauerstoffversorgung, CO2-Injektion und Kulturtechniken.

Wachsen Algen und Kieselalgen, für Gewinne. Die Märkte für Algen wächst weltweit. Spezifische Arten (Taxa) sind sehr teuer, von Anbietern, die oft

Hunderte von Dollar pro Liter zu kaufen! Bauen Sie Ihre eigene Photobioreaktor, gibt Ihnen die Mittel der wachsenden reine Monokulturen, von Algenarten, die "Ausgangsmaterial" für Ihre Algen Experimente liefern.

# Kapitel Eins - Wachsende Algen
## The Big Picture

Algen, in der Regel sind im Wasser lebende Arten. Einzel-Zell "Wachstum" Motoren, die anorganischen Materialien verbrauchen und produzieren organische Moleküle. Algen durch Photosynthese wandeln Segmente der Solarenergie, Spurenelemente, $CO_2$ und Wasser, in den erstaunlichen Prozess der "oxygenic-Photosynthese," die das Zellwachstum und Reproduktion treibt, und macht das Leben auf der Erde, wie wir es kennen, möglich.

Als Algen Grubber, Sie versuchen, die Natur nachzuahmen, und die Natur zu verbessern, durch "Auslösen" verschiedene Effekte, entlang der

"Wachstums-Zyklus," mit Ihrem Steuerbedingungen der Thermodynamik.

Photosynthese entwickelt auf der Erde, wenn das Leben brauchte eine "Batterie." Fragile DNA benötigten Schutz, mit der frühen Erde mit UV-C UV-Strahlung bombardiert, entwickelte Algen Antworten wie photosynthetische Herstellung vieler organischer Moleküle, die Überlebensreaktion der Algen erhöht.

Zubehör Pigmente, entwickelte sich die Mechanismen in den Algen, um mehr von der verfügbaren Solarstrahlung oder der Produktion von Anti-Oxidantien zu sammeln, zu "verpacken", bis das wertvolle und gefährdete DNA.

Algen vermehren während der Nacht, wahrscheinlich aufgrund der massiven Präsenz von UV-Beschuss während der Sonnenstunden, auf alten Erde.

Replizieren von DNA, in der Nacht, minimiert die Störung, die durch energiereiche Ultraviolett-(UV-) Licht in verursacht werden können,

Photobioreaktoren, wie die in diesem Buch beschrieben Satz, bieten eine Möglichkeit für Forscher, "Einfluss" der Stamm gewachsen ist, durch Veränderung der Umwelt, nach Ihren Wachstums Protokoll, für eine gewünschte Ergebnis.

## Betonend, Algen für die Produktion ausgewählt

Algen, die "hervorgehoben" werden an strategischen Zeiten in der Wachstumsphase, ausgewählt Moleküle von Interesse für den Grubber hergestellt. Ausgewählte Moleküle sind das Ziel der wachsenden Algen.

Die Algenbiomasse wird erzeugt, wenn "Energie" aus der Photosynthese diese Energien für die Zellatmung eingesetzt, und die Zellteilung "überschreiten." Die spezifische Wachstumsrate, Ihrer Algen, wird "thermodynamisch" von "wie" Sie wachsen Algen bestimmt.

Die Photobioreaktoren (PBR), hier beschrieben, können Sie den optischen, Temperaturregelung, die Rate der CO2-und O2-Flow in die Kultur anpassen, den pH-Wert und Nährstoffmischung, durch das, was Sie zu Ihrem Wachstum Gefäße hinzufügen und das "Timing , "und" rate ", an dem Sie ernten.

Bearbeiten von Nährstoffen, die Intensitäten, die Auswahl der Wellenlängen und Photoperioden, in Ihrem Lichtquelle, Temperatur, pH-Wert, gelösten CO2-und O2-Ebenen, haben dramatische Auswirkungen auf das Algenstoffwechsels.

Die spezifische Algenwachstumsrate ist die Rate-of-Change, Algenbiomasseakkumulation. Die Rate der "anabole" Prozesse (Photosynthese) und "katabolen"-Prozesse (Atmung) werden Ihren Nettogewinn Biomasse zu bestimmen.

Bearbeiten von Nährstoffen, Ebenen von Licht (photosynthetische Photonenflussdichte, PPFD), Photoperiode, Temperatur, pH und gelösten O2 und CO2-Werte, dramatische und Controlling Auswirkungen auf das Algenstoffwechsels.

Photobioreaktoren, Forschern erlauben, Wachstum Protokolle zu testen, durch die systematische Anpassung wichtigsten thermodynamischen Parameter, wie Temperatur, Lichtstufe, Photoperiode, wie beschrieben, und ist ein nützliches Werkzeug für die Forschung und Vermarktung.

Algen, verwenden häufig die Primär Pigment Chlorophyll-a. Gefunden in der gesamten Phytoplankton Reich, Chrolophyll-a ist wahrscheinlich das wertvollste Leben geben Molekül auf der Erde.

Algen haben "Secondary Pigments", die Leitungs anderen Wellenlängen im Spektrum um chemische Prozesse zu fahren entwickelt. Andere Pigmente, um zusätzliche Wellenlängen im Sonnenspektrum teh zu reagieren, und geben Sie eine Algen aufgenommen mittels Konverter für Energie, um zu überleben. Algen, ernten diese zusätzliche Sonnenspektrum, um zusätzliche Energie für den Stoffwechsel, Atmung, und die Zellteilung zu gewinnen.

Sekundäre Pigmente oder oft auch als "Zubehör" Pigmente enthalten Chlorophyll-b, Chlorophyll-c, Carotinoide und Phycobiliproteinen. Zusätzliche Pigmente bieten einen evolutionären Vorteil, thermodynamisch, zu der Algenzelle. Unsere, Vorteil ist, können wir die wertvolle "Metaboliten," und Produkte, die von diesen zusätzlichen Wege führen zu ernten.

Sekundär Pigmente, liefern die Algen mit wertvollen Molekülen, wie Anti-Oxidantien. Hohe UV-Strahlung sowie chemische Belastungen, drohte die DNA der frühen Algen. Das Protein Astaxanthin, hoch geschätzt, wurde durch die Algen entwickelt, um "Sun Block" durch eine hohe Absorptions von UV-Licht sein.

Algen, Astaxanthin, (hell in der Farbe rot), die sich nach dem Wickeln um die DNA-Proteine, um die wertvolle Fracht schützen die UV absorbiert erzeugen würde. Wenn chemische oder UV-Belastung kam der Algenzelle, entwickelte sich ein Weg, um Astixanthin produzieren, um die Zelle zu schützen.

Algen, sind extrem empfindlich, um ihren Zustand und Änderungen (Änderungsraten), um ihre Umgebungen. Die Kontrolle dieser Bedingungen, mit der Photobioreaktor, damit Sie Ihre Algen, um spezifische Moleküle von Interesse zu beeinflussen.

## Balancieren Sie in allen Dingen

Photobioreaktor, beginnt mit einem Beleuchtungssystem. Foto-autotrophs, reagieren sehr stark auf optische Energie. Der einflussreichste Aspekt der wachsenden Algen ist die optische Regime Sie in Ihrem Wachstum Protokoll verwenden. Die optische Wellenlängen-Regime richtet, Intensitäten und Photoperioden.

Chlorophyll-a, reagiert auf bestimmte Wellenlängen des Lichts, während sekundäre Pigmente auf andere Wellenlängen reagieren.

Photobioreaktoren eine Plattform bieten, um spezifische Arten (Taxa) wachsen und entwickeln Wachstum Protokolle zum natürlichen Algen Produktivität zu verbessern. Wie Sie Ihre Photobioreaktor zu verwenden, mit einem Zeitplan für die Aktionen, Messungen und Ernten Sie auswählen, bestimmt die Ausbeute.

Algen produzieren viele wertvolle Verbindungen entscheidend für Kosmetika und Nahrungsergänzungsmarkt. Die natürlichen Öle und Fette, die reich an Omega 3 Fettsäuren, und hoch geschätzt. Der menschliche Körper ist mit Algen entwickelt, und von Algen. Die natürlichen Öle und Antioxidationsmittel, nicht so oft zurückgewiesen, im Vergleich zu synthetischen Produkten für den Verbraucher.

"Haematococcus pluvialis," ein Chlorophyceae (Grünalgen), produziert mehr Antioxidans Astaxanthin, etwa 40.000 ppm, wenn "betonte:" als jede bekannte Organismus auf der Erde. Das macht (H. p.), Sehr wertvoll für die Nahrungsergänzungsmittel und kosmetische Märkten.

Astaxanthin hat einen Marktwert, in die Tausende von Dollar pro Pfund, und in den Nahrungsergänzungs ihighly und Aquakultur Märkte bewertet.

Algen, haben unglaubliche Mechanismen, um die Produktion von Photosyntheseprodukten zu verbessern, wenn "betont." Algen Biomasse Wachstum hat Ernährungs-und andere müssen Sie während der Algenwachstumszyklus manipulieren kann, um die gewünschten Bio-Produkte zu produzieren. Betonend, Algen, zunimmt oder abnimmt, was die Algen Bedürfnisse während seines Lebenszyklus.

Betonend, verändert sich die Umgebung der Algen, um eine vorhergesagte Reaktion, wie die Produktion von Astaxanthin zu produzieren.

Der Photobioreaktor Kit, wie unten beschrieben, stellt die Ausrüstung, die Sie brauchen, um zu wachsen, und Einfluss, Wachstumsprofil Ihres Algen.

Algen haben sehr reaktions "Stoffwechsel" Sie beeinflusst zu höheren Ebenen der ausgewählten

Bio-Produkte, darunter Aminosäuren, Proteine, Bio-Farbstoffe, Antioxidantien, Vitamine, und wichtig für die Produktion von Biokraftstoffen produzieren: Lipide.

Lipide (Öle), sind das Prinzip Rohstoff für Biodiesel (sowohl Pflanzen-und tierischen Fett-Säuren können als Ausgangsmaterial verwendet werden). Fatty-Säuren, können in Biodiesel umgeestert werden.

Die von Algen produzierten Lipide, werden oft als "Speicher" Lipide (nicht-polaren) und "strukturelle" Lipide (polare Lipide) kategorisiert. "Storage" Typ Lipide, große Triaclglycerides (TAGS), kann Biodiesel hergestellt transesterefied werden.

Forscher haben untersucht Einflussalgenzellen für die Biodieselproduktion von "Begrenzung" eine Variable in der Wachstumszyklus. "Tricking" die Algen, indem eine Bedingung, die Produktion eines gewünschten "Molekül" Produktion zu induzieren, da ein Teil der erzeugten Biomasse. Photobioreaktoren (PBR), damit die Algen Grubber Bedingungen, wie Temperatur, pH-Wert, Lichtverhältnisse, das Vorhandensein oder Fehlen von chemischen Nährstoffen, um eine gewünschte Ausgabe zu erzeugen einzustellen.

Alles Leben auf der Erde, mit wenigen Ausnahmen, abhängig von sauerstoff-Photosynthese, als der primäre Prozess, der Ernährung produziert (für die Basis der Nahrungskette) und Sauerstoff.

Photosynthese, ist der "Primärproduzent" aller Nahrung und Sauerstoff, auf denen das Leben auf der Erde und die Ozeane ab. Die "Stromversorgung" für die Photosynthese, die Sonne und liefert eine Spitzenleistung an der Oberfläche der Erde von 1.000 Watt / Quadratmeter.

Um die Photosynthese zu stimulieren, müssen Sie die Wellenlängen, die die Antworteigenschaften der Algen Primäre und sekundäre Pigmente beherrschen zu produzieren. Jede Algen, müssen ihre besonderen Sweet Spot aller thermodynamischen Faktoren.

# Kapitel Zwei - Auswählen Ihrer Algen Dehnungs

Kaufen Monokulturen (reine Arten), von Algen ist teuer - oft Hunderte von Dollar pro Liter!

Photo-Bioreaktoren können verwendet werden, um Algen Monokulturen wachsen und zu speichern, über die Zeit, möglicherweise Tausende von Dollar in Algenkultivierungskosten werden.

Algen-Spezies von Interesse, werden ausgewählt, weil Sie eine bestimmte oder mehrere Moleküle der Wert ein. Auswählen Algen, ist, das Problem zu arbeiten "Rücklauf." Start, mit dem, was Sie am Ende mit nach Wachstum wollen. Die Arten (Taxa) Sie sich entscheiden, hängt davon ab, was Sie als Endprodukt produzieren wollen. Sie suchen nach Öle, (Lipide), für die Biodiesel-oder Kosmetikindustrie? Sie suchen für eine vollständige Proteine (essentielle Aminosäuren), für die Fischfutter-Markt?

Ihre Wahl der Algen hängt von Ihren Zielen. Die folgende Liste von Algen, beispielsweise, sind mit einer Reihe von Lipidgehalt (Trockengewicht) aufgeführt. Jede Spezies (Taxa) hat ein eigenes Protokoll Wachstum und Wachstumsraten. Lipidgehalt des Algen Chargen hängen von Ihrer Anbautechnik, wie Sie zu impfen, und starten Sie Ihre Kultur, das Wachstumsmedium, das Sie Ihre Glasgefäße Wachstum hinzufügen, wird die Lichtregime Sie sich bewerben, und wie gut Sie steuern, pH-Wert und Temperatur.

Das folgende ist eine Liste von nützlichen und wertvollen Algenarten (Taxa):

**Chlorella vulgaris**

**Chlorella minotissima**

**Ankistrodesmus sp.**

**Crypthecodinium cohnii**

**Scenedesmus sp.**

**Cyclotella sp.**

**Dunaliella tertiolecta**

**Hantzchia sp.**

**Nannochloropsis**

**Neochloris oleoabundans**

**Nitzschia sp.**

**Phaeodactylum tricornutum**

**Stichococcus sp.**

**Nannochloris**

**Thalassiosira pseudonana**

**Tetraselmis suecica**

**Botryococcus branuii**

Der Superstar Chlorella vulgaris - ist bekannt für seine hohe Produktivität untersucht.  Algen

Biodiesel auf Basis von Chlorella vulgaris hat Vorteile in Bezug auf die hohen Wachstumsraten bieten, und einige Probleme angegangen werden, einschließlich der ziemlich hart Zellulosezellwand, die "gebrochen", um die internen Öle zu erreichen sein muss.

Chlorella vulgaris, ein Chlorophyceae, wächst gut mit bekannten Verhältnisse der Nährstoffe C: N: P: K Begrenzung Stickstoff (Verhältnis zu anderen Nährstoffen) und Chlorella vulgaris reagiert, produziert mehr Stärken, und mehrfach ungesättigten Fettsäure-Lipiden.

Mehrfach ungesättigte Fettsäuren-Säuren, sind eine große Auszeichnung. Die "nährstoff begrenzt" Algen spüre eine kleine Krise, und produzieren mehr Lipide auf "speichern" Energie für eine voraussichtliche Defizit.

Wenn Sie die Wahl eines Algenstamm für mehrfach ungesättigte Fettsäure-Lipid-Produktion, Chlorella vulgaris ist eine gute Wahl. Chlorella minotissima, aus dem Phylum Chlorophyta, wenn Stickstoff begrenzt produziert 39% EPA (Omega-3-Fettsäure-Eicosapentaensäure-Säure in Nahrungsergänzungsmittel hoch geschätzt, und Biodieselmärkten.

Nannochloropsis, zeigt große Algen Biodiesel-Produktion als durch Nährstoffbegrenzung "beeinflusst". Nannochloropsis wird von sechs identifizierten Taxa, jede vielversprechende zusammengesetzt ist, und leben in Salzwasser, Frischwasser und Brackwasser.

Nannochloropsis, unter den richtigen Bedingungen gewachsen ist, kann bis zu 60% Trockengewicht von mehrfach ungesättigten Fettsäuren-Säuren ansammeln, in Stickstoff-Wachstum begrenzt Protokolle. Dies macht Nannochloropsis hoch geschätzt, als potenzielle Einsatzmaterial in der Biokraftstoffindustrie.

# Kapitel Drei - Bauen Sie Ihr eigenes Photobioreaktor

Sie können Ihre PBR bauen mit 4 Glas Wachsende Schiffe. Sie erhalten eine PVC-Rahmen zu bauen, und legen Sie zwei Leuchtstoff-Leuchten auf der Oberseite der PVC-Rahmen über den wachsenden Gefäße. Sie werden Aquarienpumpen in die Luft zu pumpen und CO2 in die Gefäße zu platzieren. Die Schiffe haben "Stopfen" in der oberen 2-Loch-Typ.

Ihr Foto-Bioreaktor-System einbinden:

Heavy Duty Timer, Mechanische Rahmen, aus PVC-Rohren von Hardware-Geschäft gemacht.

Vier (4) 20 Liter Wachstum Schiffe. Glas Wachstum Schiffe mit 100% Non-Toxic Food-Grade Schlauch, Stecker und Armaturen.

Pneumatische Luftpumpen mit Inline Bakterienfilter für sterile Belüftung und Durchmischung, mit "Pasteur Kurve" Austrittsöffnungen, um eine Kontamination zu verhindern Taxa

Einfach zu montieren und zu desinfizieren für verschiedene Taxa Serien.

Ausgelegt für 80 Liter, die vier Behälter PBR (je 20 Liter), verwendet werden, die alle für eine Monokultur von Algen Taxa. Sie können auch jedes Gefäß verwenden, um völlig unterschiedliche und separate Taxa wachsen - bis zu vier verschiedene Taxa mit diesem Algen wachsen-Kit.

Jedes Glas wachsenden Gefäß ist unabhängig von den anderen Schiffen, mit ihren eigenen Bakterienfilter und "Pasteur Kurve" Abluftöffnungen.

Komplette Photobioreaktor (PBR) Kit enthält:

Mechanische Elemente
Pneumatikelemente
Biologische Filterelemente
Optische Elemente
Elektrische Absicherung / Photoperiode Timer-System

Biologische Filter für jedes Schiff, sterilisieren Luftstrom in Ihrem Kulturgefäße, und "Pasteur Kurve" Ausgangsöffnungen, verbieten Kontamination in Ihre Kulturgefäße Strom zurück.

Verwenden Sie Glas, Pyrex Glasröhren und 100% ungiftig Food-Grade Material für empfindliche Bauteile.

Komplette Optical System produziert PAR-Licht mit über 200 micro-moles/m2/sec Photonenflussdichte, durch Auswechseln der Lampe höhenverstellbar und verfügt mit Heavy Duty Timer. Die Kits enthalten auch alle Gläser und Armaturen, Druckluftluftpumpen, Maschinenbau-Rahmen, Fused Elektrische Anlage - Alles, was Sie brauchen (Hardware) zu wachsen beginnen Algenkulturen.

Alle PBR Algen wachsen Kits beinhalten Non-Toxic Verdunstungs Sanitizer für wiederholte Anbau DIY Photobioreaktor PBR Algen wachsen Kit enthält:

Zwei (2) High-Efficiency T8 Leuchtstofflampe Auflast Leuchten, Vier (4) 6500K High-Efficiency-Lampen (20.000 Stunden). Ein (1) Heavy Duty Timer (Stecker die Lampen in den Timer zu Ihrem Photoperiode festgelegt).

Ein (1) Heavy Duty Fused Power Strip.

Ein (1) Mechanische Rahmen Kit. Vorgeschnittene und Ausgestattet für einfache Montage. Die "mechanischen" Rahmen ist aus PVC-Rohren zusammengesetzt (3/4 "bis 1,5" wählen Sie) erhältlich im Baumarkt. Schneiden Sie Stücke wie folgt:

Acht (8) Längenabschnitte (18" jeweils)
Acht (8) die Seitensegmente (22" jeweils)
Six (6) Vertikalsegmente (20" jeweils)
Acht (8) 3-Way Corner Steckverbinder
Acht (8) 3-Way Mittel Steckverbinder

Baut in Rahmung wie oben gezeigt. Die Frame unterstützt die Lichter, und "definiert" einen Innenraum, wo die wachsende Schiffe im Rahmen der Lampen platziert.

Vier (4) Glas Wachsende Schiffe bei 20 Liter Kapazität Each bewertet.

Vier (4) Pyrex Glasrohre für die Belüftung Eingang in die Wachstums Kulturen.

Vier (4) 100% Non-Toxic Food-Grade Wachstum Fahrzeug Top Dichtungen / Schläuche / Einbausätze

Vier (4) 100% Non-Toxic Food-Grade "Pasteur Curve" Auspuff Vents

Zwei (2) High-Efficiency Luftpumpen (4000 cm$^3$ / min) über vier Wachstums Schiffe. Bringen Sie einen "Splitter," so dass Sie zwei Gefäße belüften, unabhängig von einer Luftpumpe.

Vier (4) Check-Ventile (um die Luftpumpen zu schützen)

Vier (4) Inline Bakterienfilter (eine für jede Wachstumsbehälter) bei 0,22 &mgr; bewertet.

Legen Sie die Inline-Bakterienfilter zwischen der Luftpumpe, und jedes Wachstum des Schiffes.

Twenty Two feet (22 '), 100% Non-Toxic Food-Grade Schlauchleitung

Ein (1) Liter Verdunstungs Sanitizer Lösung 100% Non-Toxic Food-Grade

Insgesamt Kit enthält (96) Teile.

Nennleistung: 148 Watt

Kosten zu bedienen: Weniger als 2 Cent pro Stunde (bei 12 Cent / kWh Stromtarife)
Footprint: 8 Quadratmeter, Höhe: 3 Meter, Breite: 2 Meter, Länge: 4 Meter, Gewicht: 57 £

# Kapitel Vier - Algen Optics

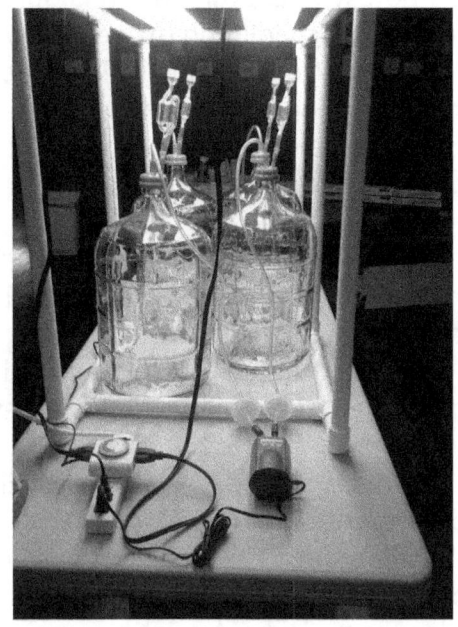

Photon-Wellenlängen, Intensitäten und Photoperioden sind von entscheidender Bedeutung, wie Algen brauchen eine Bedingung "Goldilocks" exponentielles Wachstum erreichen.

In allzu viel Lichtenergie und Sie veranlassen werde "Lichtsättigung." Lichtsättigung, ist, wenn Sie die Foto-Reaktionszentren in den Zellen überlastet habe, und nicht mehr Licht kann den Prozess zu fahren. In der Tat, wenn Sie "Lichtsättigung" Bedingungen zu erreichen, dann werden Sie hemmen die Photosynthese ist dieser Effekt Light-Hemmung.

In allzu wenig Photonenintensität, und Sie werden die Netto-Photosynthese für "Entschädigung" Punkt nicht erreicht. Entschädigung ist, wenn Ihr Algen produzieren einen Nettogewinn in Algenbiomasse. Diese "Entschädigung Punkt" ist, wo die Photosynthese für die Atmung und die Zellteilung notwendige Energie übersteigt.

Algen wachsen, wenn Photonenintensität ist zwischen der "Kompensationspunkt" und die "Lichtsättigung" Punkt in der Wachstumskurve. Hinweis: einer der größten Fehler, die von Algen Bauern gemacht ist, allzu viel Licht zu verwenden.

Thermodynamisch, sobald Sie "Sättigung" Ebenen mit der Lichtintensität zu erreichen - keine zusätzlichen Photonen zu dem System hinzugefügt wird den Prozess weiter oder schneller zu fahren und. Stellen Sie die Höhe des Rahmens, um die Intensität des Lichts einzustellen.

Verwenden Sie ein Quantum Meter, wenn möglich, genau zu messen, photosynthetisch aktiven Strahlung (PAR) von 400 nm bis 700 nm, Leistungsdichte in der Mikro-Mol Photonen (Mikro-Einsteins) / m2/second. Foto-Zeiten sind entscheidend für wachsende Algen. Die Tages Tag-Nacht-Zyklus ist eine grundlegende Einfluss darauf, wie Algen entwickelt.

Ihre Wahl der Photoperioden haben dramatische Auswirkungen auf den Lebenszyklus von Algen, wie jede Art hat ihre bevorzugten Tag-Nacht-Zyklus.

LED-Technologie ist es den Forschern erlaubt, die "Emissionsgrad" der LED-Strahler auf die "Absorptionsfähigkeit" der primären und sekundären Pigmente in Algen entsprechen. Allerdings LEDs oft nicht genau mit der Wellenlänge "peak" Reaktion einiger Pigmente.

New Organische LEDs (OLED) können LED Emissions zu sein "abstimmbare" und einrasten genaue Pigment Peak-Wellenlängen. Die Annahme der LED-Strahler auf die wachsende Algen einen hohen Wirkungsgrad (Sie nur Wellenlängen Erregen Sie benötigen) bieten, (Lauf LEDs cool) Niedertemperatur-und hohe Kontrolle über Intensität und Dauer.

Algen-Photobioreaktor Zuchtsets verwenden T-8-Lampen-Typ können Sie eine beliebige Anzahl von ausgewählten Lampen, die diesen physischen Format gerecht zu verwenden. LED-Lampen für T-8 Armaturen können online lokal beschafft werden, oder.

Verwenden Algen-Photobioreaktor wachsen Kits Algen für Biokraftstoffe zu wachsen, und die Biodieselproduktion. Biodieselproduktion mit Algen, hat enorme Marktchancen als Haupttransportindustrie Druck auf Dieselproduzenten, mehr Biodiesel zu verwenden.

Die Biodiesel-Markt ist mit Hugh-LKW, Züge, Schiffe, Landmaschinen, Baumaschinen, nicht zu vergessen, viele Autos und Lastwagen können mit Biodiesel fahren. Biodiesel aus Algen mit Wasser Abfallströme, mit überschüssigen Phosphor und Stickstoff überlastet als Nährstoffe erschlossen werden. Nährstoffe werden sehr geschätzt, vor allem Phosphor.

Biodiesel aus Algen, verwendet werden, um Wasserströme wertvoller Reinigung P: K: N kombinieren, um zwei Einnahmequellen zu erzeugen: Einkommen für die Reinigung der Umwelt, und Einkommen für Biodiesel produziert.

Algen haben "Zubehör Pigmente," wie Chlorophyll-b und-c Chlorophyll, absorbieren bei Spitzen, die sowohl in den violett-blau und orange-roten Bändern, aber leicht variiert werden. Andere Zubehör Pigmente, einschließlich Carotinoide (Beta-Carotin), absorbieren im verschobenen Wellenlänge Spitzen auf unterschiedlichen Wellenlängen als die primäre Pigment Chlorophyll-a zu erfassen.

Im Fall von Chlorophyll-a und Chlorophyll-b muss jedes "peak" gleichzeitig aktiviert werden. Jeder - zusammen - treibt einen photochemischen Weg in Photo II aktiv und Photosystem I, die die lichtabhängige Prozesse in der Photosynthese zu fahren.

Photosynthese ist in zwei separaten Teilen: lichtabhängigen Reaktionen (in den Foto-Reaktionszentren) "oxidieren" Wasser, und die lichtunabhängigen Reaktionen (Calvin-Zyklus), die "reduzieren" $CO_2$, die Bausteine aller anderen organischen Molekülen herzustellen: einfache Zucker.

Photobioreaktor Algen wachsen Kits sind für die Algenforscher entworfen. Wachsen Algen für Biodiesel und Nahrungsergänzungsmittel-Projekte. Entwicklung spezifischer pH-Wert, Temperatur, Beleuchtungsstärke, Licht Foto-Perioden, Nährstoff-Rezepte und andere Variablen, um Ihren Algen Ausgänge zu maximieren. Bei der Photosynthese Algen "oxidieren" Wasser, um ein Elektron und ein Proton zu ernten - die Freigabe Sauerstoff als Abfallprodukt Algen.

Wasser oxidiert Herstellung von einem Elektron und Proton-Paar. Einmal gebildet, werden die Ladungspartikel getrennt, wodurch ea "Potentialdifferenz," um eine Elektronenübertragungskette zu fahren, dass die Ladung zu transportieren später von der Calvin-Benson-Zyklus verwendet werden, um organische Moleküle zu bauen.

Der Calvin-Zyklus chemisch "reduziert" $CO_2$ (Carbon-Befestigung) und baut einfache Kohlenhydrate, um Energie zu speichern.

Algen haben optische Bedürfnisse. Foto Flussdichte, die Rate der Energieabgabe an Ihren Algenkultur hat Maßnahme über einen weiten Bereich von weniger als 2 Mikro Mol photons/m2/second zu einer üblichen 80-200 Mikro Mole photons/m2/sec gewesen .

Photonenenergie für den Anbau von Algen in Photobioreaktoren hat drei wesentliche Aspekte:

**Photosynthese-Wellenlängen**
**Photon Intensitäten**
**Photoperioden**

Photobioreaktor Algen wachsen Kits bieten Kontrolle über alle drei optische Faktoren. Mit T-8 universelle Lampen können verschiedene Spektren Lampen in Ihrem inbegriffen Lampe Leuchten zu erregen, um alle Arten von optischen Algenwachstum Experimente zu entwerfen.

Photobioreaktor Algenwachstum Protokolle geben Ihnen die Kontrolle über die Lichtdurchlässigkeit. Teiche und andere Outdoor-Algenwachstum Ansätze steht ein großes Problem mit "Licht-Hemmung."

Licht Hemmung tritt auf, wenn Algen wachsen auf der Oberfläche eines Teiches und Block-Licht eindringen die Wassersäule. Dieser Algenwachstum Oberfläche "Schattierungen" die Algen unter und erzeugt eine Hemmung des Wachstums.

Ein Paradoxon der wachsenden Algen in Teichen ist desto mehr wachsen, desto mehr Algen beschattet werden. Leichte Hemmung begrenzt die Produktivität von Teichen bis zu einer Tiefe von etwa 1-2 cm. Algen sind im Wasser lebende Arten, die bestimmte Umweltbedingungen zu wachsen benötigen. Dazu gehören Temperatur, pH-Wert, gelösten $CO_2$, gelöster $O_2$, Nährstoffe, Makro-und Mikr, PAR-Licht zwischen 400-700 nm und eine regelmäßige Photoperiode.

Photosynthetischen Photonenflussdichte (PPFD) beschreibt die Energieabgabe des optischen Systems. Stromdichten für die von einem bestimmten Taxa Bereich auf über 200 erforderlich durch Arten weniger als 2 Mikro Mole photons/m2/ second, für Arctic Algen PAR Licht Mikro-Mole photons/m2/second für weitere typische Algenarten.

PBR-Kits sind für eine Nenn 300 micro-moles/m2/ sec von PAR Licht zu erzeugen. Diesen Betrag können Sie je nach Einstellung der Höhe Ihrer Lichtanlage.

Algen wachsen Kits beinhalten den kompletten Rahmung, Beleuchtungssystem, Servosteuerungssystem, Glas-und Pyrexglas wachsenden Gefäßen, Bakterienfilter, "Pasteur Kurven" und Air Pumping-System. Photobioreaktor Kits sind für Sie entwickelt, Algen Monokulturen wertvoller Algen wachsen.

Algen sind mit Chloroplasten (mit den Photostellen) ausgestattet und treten in aller Zelloberfläche. Licht in einen Wassersäule entweder absorbiert oder gebeugt, wie es fährt. Partikel im Wasser, einschließlich Algen, streuen das Licht, das nicht absorbiert wird. Streulicht ist ein Vorteil gegenüber Algen, wie es "normalisiert," die Photonen Richtung und ermöglicht es den Zellen zu erfassen und zu nutzen Photonen aus allen Richtungen.

Photonen in Wasser wird "Scatter" und "absorbieren" in alle Richtungen einschließlich wieder, so dass Licht in Wasser ein sehr aktives Profil von bis Welling und unten quillt Normalisierung Photonenpfade - Abend des Lichts (Photonen-) Verteilung innerhalb der Algen Wassersäule

Foto-Zeiten sind entscheidend für wachsende Algen. Die Tages Tag-Nacht-Zyklus ist ein grundlegender Einfluss darauf, wie Algen entwickelt. Photoperioden haben dramatische Auswirkungen auf den Lebenszyklus von Algen und jede Art hat seine bevorzugte Tag-Nacht-Zyklus.

Die meisten Algenwachstum auftritt, mit einem 12-Stunden und 12-Stunden-Photoperiode aus. Verlängerung oder Verkürzung der Verhältnis hat jedoch Auswirkungen auf die Zellphysiologie und Reaktion. Wenn "Sonnenstunden" nehmen zu, die Alge wissen, dass der Sommer kommt und erhöht die photosynthetischen Reaktion.

Wenn Sie "Sonnenstunden," Algen reagieren zu verkürzen "kommenden Winter" produziert mehr Lipiden. Algen für Biodiesel bietet eine wirkliche Quelle von Kohlenstoff-neutrale Kraftstoffe. Algen für Biodiesel kann mit Abwasserströme aus der Landwirtschaft angebaut werden, und Vieh Quellen mit echten Klimaneutralität. Kohle für das Algenwachstum kommt aus der Atmosphäre und wird in die Atmosphäre zurückgeführt, wenn verbraucht.

Photosynthese-Pigmente sind Proteine zur Verfügung zu bestimmten Photonenenergie von entscheidender Bedeutung für die Photosynthese zu erfassen.

Licht (Photonen-Energie) ist der wichtigste Faktor für den Anbau von Algen zu berücksichtigen. (Obwohl alle thermodynamischen Bedingungen wichtig sind). Photosynthese ist die primäre Antriebsmechanismus Algenwachstum und seine Bedeutung im Handel wächst Algen dominant ist. Algen erfordern spezifische Wellenlänge der Photonenenergie im Bereich von 400 nm bis 700 nm auf.

Photosynthetisch aktiven Strahlung (PAR) Licht bezieht sich auf das breite Spektrum von Wellenlängen, auf die Pigmente reagieren auch nicht einer "Oktave" von Lichtfrequenzen -ein sehr schmales Band All oxygene Photosynthese auf der Erde wird von Wellenlängen zwischen 400 nm und

700 nm angetrieben angesichts der großen elektromagnetischen Spektrums.

Der primäre Pigment in der ganzen Welt verwendet wird, Algen Chlorophyll-a. Chlorophyll-a, vielleicht ist das wichtigste Molekül auf dem Planeten, wegen seiner Fähigkeit, diese Photonen, die von der Photoreaktion Centers II benötigt, zu erfassen, und ich, der Photosynthese Licht fahren abhängigen Reaktionen.

Sekundäre Pigmente wie Chlorophyll-b, Chlorophyll-c, Carotinoide, und Phycobiliproteinen sind Proteine, die Erfassung und absorbieren ausgewählt Photonen. Energizing eine "Kaskade" von Reaktionen dieser photonischen Capture-Funktion ist am wichtigsten. Maximieren Sie Ihre Algen Pigmente durch die Stimulierung sowohl "Spitzen" in ihren Absorptionsspektren.

Photobioreaktor Algenwachstum Kits können Sie die optischen Bedingungen wie Intensität der photosynthetisch aktiven Strahlung (PAR) Licht wichtig in wachsenden Algen steuern. Photosynthese Algen arbeitet über einen weiten Bereich von Bedingungen abhängig von der Spezies, aber die Wellenlängen und Intensitäten der Photonenenergie sind, thermodynamisch am wichtigsten.

Algen wachsen mit PAR Licht im Bereich von 400 nm bis 700 nm Wellenlängen. Intensitäten PAR Licht variieren von weniger als 2 Mikro Mole photons/m2/sec für arktische Algen zu 200 Mikro-Mole photons/m2/sec für mehr gemeinsame Algenarten. Jede Spezies wird eine bevorzugte Photonenintensität, Sammlung aktive Wellenlängen und Photoperiode haben, ein Licht-und Dunkel-Zyklus zu ermöglichen.

Die genauen Wellenlängen Algen in oxygene Photosynthese zu nutzen, hängt von der primären Pigment (Chlorophyll-a), die zwei Absorptionspeaks, ein in den violett-blau und Gipfel wieder in der orange-roten Teil des Spektrums hat.

# Kapitel Fünf - Algen Ernährung

Wachsende Algen, hängt von vielen Faktoren, einschließlich der Nährmedium Sie für Ihre spezifische Arten (Taxa) zu wählen.

Begrenzung Nährstoffe, wie Stickstoff, wirkt sich in vielen Algenarten, mehr Lipide zu produzieren. Forscher nutzen diese Nährstoff-und andere Faktor Einschränkungen, die Algen zu stimulieren, um eine gewünschte Bio-Produkt zu erzeugen. Chlorella vulgaris wird gut kennen, um deutlich mehr Lipide zu produzieren, und Stärken als Stickstoff beschränkt.

Photobioreaktor (PBR) Algen wachsen Kits ein Werkzeug für die Algenforscher auf bestimmte Nährstoffmischungen, die Wachstumsraten und Netto-Algenbiomasseproduktion erhöhen entwerfen.

Algen, Kieselalgen und Cyanobakterien erfordern Makro-und Mikronährstoffe, gelöste Ionen, Spurenmetalle und verschiedene Vitamine. Gedeihen Wachstumsmedien für Algen werden in Abhängigkeit von Süßwasser oder Salzwasserarten gruppiert. Es gibt keine universelle Wachstumsmedien Rezept, das für alle funktioniert Taxa, so Untersuchungen sind gezwungen, sehr darauf, wie Wachstumsmedien zusammensetzt geben, gespeichert und genutzt werden.

**Algenwachstum Medien Rezepte**

Makronährstoffe durch Algen, Kieselalgen, Blaualgen und erforderlich sind, umfassen Kohlenstoff, Stickstoff, Phosphor, Silicium und große Ionen, einschließlich Na, K, Mg, Ca, Cl und SO4 als Basismedien.

Mikronährstoffe sind Spurenmengen von wesentlichen Elementen, und diese umfassen Eisen, Mangan, Zink, Kobalt, Kupfer, Molybdän, und eine kleine Menge von Metalloid Selen.

Vitamine - sind entscheidend für das Wachstum von Algen, insbesondere drei: Vitamin B1 (Thiamini - HCL), Vitamin B12 (Cyanocolbalamin) und Vitamin H (Biotin) Viele Algen brauchen nur ein oder zwei, je nach Art, aber es scheint keine zu sein schaden Sie sich mit der alle drei.

Der Zusatz von Spurenelementen sind eine heikle Angelegenheit in Algenkultivierung. Nur geringe Mengen an Spurenmetalle, wie Eisen, Kupfer, Zink und Kobalt, sind für die Photosynthese-Prozesse. Hinweis: Alle Spurenelemente sind giftig für Algen, wenn Konzentrationen zu hoch sind. Große Vorsicht ist geboten mit milli-grams/Liter nicht zu verwechseln micro-grams/Liter werden.

Das Element Eisen - wird von allen Phytoplankton benötigt, als dies der wesentliche Stoffwechselfunktionen im Elektronentransport.

Das Element Mangan - eine wesentliche Komponente der Wasser oxidierenden Zentren der Photosynthese.

Das Element Zink -. Wie Mangan wird durch Algen, Kieselalgen und Cyanobakterien für eine Vielzahl von Stoffwechselfunktionen verwendet Eine wichtige Verwendung von Zink ist an der Bildung von "Carboanhydrase" - so essentielles Enzym ist entscheidend für den $CO_2$-Transport und Kohlenstoff-Fixierung.

Das wesentliche Element Kupfer - ist wegen seiner Funktion im "Cytochrom-Oxidase", vital für alle Phytoplankton Leben - ein essentielles Protein in der Algenzelle Atemelektronentransport.

Wachstumsmedien Nährstoff Rezepte sind sowie diejenigen, einer Meisterkoch in der Kochkunst bewacht.

Entwickeln Sie Ihre eigenen Rezepte und entdecken Sie die perfekte Mischung von Nährstoffen zu exponentiellem Wachstum der Algen zu fahren.

Süßwasseralgenarten verwenden in der Regel Wachstumsmedien in drei große Unterkategorien unterteilt: synthetische, angereichert, und Boden-Wasser. Synthetische Wachstumsmedien ist "künstlich" Medien von den Algen Forscher entwickelt, um eine vereinfachte und spezifisch definierten Medien. Beispiele dafür sind "die Bold Basal Medium," Chu # 10-Medium, BG-11-Medium, Medium und WC.

Es ist eine große Kunst bei der Vorbereitung Süßwasserwachstumsmedien für Algen - sicher sein, nicht zu Leitungswasser oder destilliertem Wasser zu verwenden. Spurenmetallverunreinigungen in Leitungs und destilliertem Wasser kann Ihr Algen vergiften. Angereichertes Wachstumsmedium wird durch Zugabe von Nährstoffen auf Naturstrom oder Seewasser, durch die Anreicherung oder eine "synthetische" Medien mit Boden-oder Pflanzenextrakte hergestellt. Angereicherten Medium ist nicht definiert, da der unbekannte organische und anorganische Verbindungen enthalten.

Algen Pioneer Redfield (1938) beschreibt Methoden für die Aufbewahrung Dauerkulturen isoliert von marinen Kieselalgen - reich an Omega-3-Fettsäuren - in großen Mengen für seine Laborexperimente.

Redfield Verfahren einbezogen strategisch Erntealgenbiomasse an einem bestimmten Punkt in der exponentiellen Wachstumsphase. Mengen von Kilogramm Trockenmasse wurden Kieselalgen kultiviert und geerntet, für seine Labor-und Aquakulturexperimente.

Redfield ist in der Biologie berühmt, für die "Redfield-Verhältnis" der photosynthetischen Zusammensetzung wichtig für Nährstoffmischung Rezepte, verwendet werden, um Algen wachsen. Redfield-Verhältnis von 106 Kohlenstoff: 16 Stickstoff: 1 Phosphor ist ein Eckpfeiler der Algenwachstum Protokolle und geändert wurde, von vielen Forschern, um Trace-Metall-Ionen, die für dynamische Algenwachstum erforderlich sind, enthalten.

Algen-Photobioreaktor Wachstums-Kits ein Instrument zur Messung von Algenbiomasse Wachstumsraten und Wachstum beträgt über direkt wachsenden Algen.

Wachsende Algen erfordert vom Management, Planung und Durchführung eines bestimmten Wachstums Protokoll.

Algenarten haben sehr spezifische Appetit Wachstumsmedien, und es ist nicht universell Nährstoffmischung, die für alle Arten funktioniert gleichermaßen. Daher Forscher Photobioreaktoren zum photo Wachstum in einer steuerbaren Umgebung steuern.

Mit Boden-Wasser-Medien Verfahren zur Anreicherung eines Wachstumsmedien mit natürlichen Elementen im Boden gefunden. Wählen Sie als "saubere" einen Boden wie möglich. Wählen Sie nicht Ton, und trocknen Sie das Material bei schwacher Hitze.

Wenn es trocken ist, durch ein Sieb laufen und sichten den Boden in kleine Partikel. In den Wasser und lassen sich am Boden. Natürliche Diffusion wesentlich Huminstoffe und Eigenschaften in der Erde einschließlich pH-Wert, Leitfähigkeit, organische Puffer, Nährstoffe und Vitamine zu diffundieren zu lassen in die Wachstumsmedien.

Photobioreaktor PBR Algen wachsen Kits erlauben Ihnen, mit Nährstoff-Protokolle experimentieren und wachsen Algen. Entwickeln Sie Ihre eigenen Nährstoff Rezepte für die spezifischen Algen Sie wachsen wollen.

Wasserqualität ist der wichtigste Ausgangspunkt bei der Gestaltung Ihrer Nährmedium. dH2O bezieht sich allgemein auf destilliertes oder deionisiertes Wasser. Verwenden Sie keine dH2O (destilliertes) Wasser, weil der aktuelle Trace-Ionen-Verunreinigungen.

Mit Reverse-Osmose-Wasser oder Glas destilliertem Wasser für einen Ausgangspunkt für Ihre synthetischen Medien Rezepte. Nährstoffmischungen werden dann zusammengesetzt, um das Wasser im Autoklaven sterilisieren, bevor Sie Algen Impfmittel einzuführen.

# Kapitel Sechs - Algen für Biokraftstoffe

**"Der Einsatz von Pflanzenölen für Kraftstoffen mag heute unbedeutend, aber solche Öle können sich im Laufe der Zeit ebenso wichtig wie Erdöl und Kohle-Teer-Produkte von der Gegenwart." (Rudolf Diesel - 1912)**

Die Flüssigkraftstoffmarkt, in den USA allein mehr als $1,8 Milliarden pro Tag. Knacken Sie die Algenöl speichernden Protokolle und die Märkte mit Kohlenstoff-neutrale Kraftstoffe Algen abgegriffen werden.

Öl-Algen ansammeln und Kieselalgen, sind der Schlüssel zu großen Algenbasis Biokraftstoffe Biodiesel und Märkten.

Kieselalgen und Algen können mit Photobioreaktoren gezüchtet werden. Algen, als der primäre Rohstoff für Biokraftstoffe und Biodiesel, mit produktiven Öl-Algen ansammeln erreicht, in ihrer ruhenden oder Ruhezustand. Verwenden Sie Photobioreaktor PBR-Kits, um Algen zu wachsen, und führen Sie Ihre eigene Experimente Algen Bio-Produkte zu erhöhen.

Wachsende Algen für Biodiesel stellt die größte Marktchance des 21. Jahrhunderts einschließlich Transport-Kraftstoffe Biodiesel sind ein Multi-Milliarden-Dollar-Markt täglich. Algen Biodiesel mit dieser Entwicklung erfordert mehr als 80 Millionen Barrel täglich Pflanzenölproduktion  Algen für Biodiesel kann diese erzeugen High-Volume, weil unsere organische Abfallströme weit über diesen Wert.

Algen für Biodiesel macht ein starkes wirtschaftliches Argument, Wasserverschmutzung Abfallströme enthalten die meisten Nährstoffe benötigt, um Algen im großen Maßstab wachsen. Wasser Wege sind mit Stickstoff, Phosphor, Kalium und andere Elemente in unserer Wasserverschmutzungsquellen überbetont. Algen für biodisel reinigen können, (Carbon neutral) und "behandeln" das Wasserverschmutzung Herstellung sauberer Wasser-und Biodiesel-Kraftstoff. Wasserverschmutzung kann "umgeleitet", um Algen für die Biodieselproduktion gleichzeitig lösen zwei Probleme wachsen.

Organische Abfälle-Dämpfe derzeit "abgeschoben" zu fragilen Wasserwege als die Hauptnahrungsquelle für den Anbau von Algen Biodiesel erschlossen werden. Können Algen Biodiesel in vielen Orten mit lokalen Bio-Abfallströme Erhöhung der Energiesicherheit für die auf Algenbasis hergestellt werden Biodiesel-Netzwerke .

Sie können Algenarten für ihre Lipid-Ausgang für Biodiesel Ausgangsmaterial auswählen. Wenn Ihr Interesse Ethanol, dann für eine besonders stärkehaltige Stamm suchen.

**Wachsende Algen für die Biodieselproduktion beginnt mit bestimmten Algen Biodiesel Wachstum Protokolle**

Photobioreaktor (PBR) Algen wachsen Kits sind für den Anbau von Algen unter Ihrem Wachstum Protokolle, um organische Moleküle von Interesse ausgelegt. Algen Biodiesel auf Basis versucht, die Wasserverschmutzung Ressourcen (N, P, K) übernehmen und leiten sie als Rohstoff für Biodiesel, um Algen zu produzieren .

Photobioreaktor Algen wachsen Kits ermöglichen es Ihnen, die wichtigsten thermodynamischen Parameter variieren. Kontrollieren Lichtstärke, Wellenlängen, Foto-Perioden, Wachstums Nährmedien, pneumatische Be-und Algenarten.

Viele Algen Anbautechniken existieren und beschrieben worden, um "schubsen" Algen, um mehr von dem, was Sie wollen. Algen für Biodiesel sucht ungesättigten Lipidproduktion - zur Herstellung von Biodiesel am effizientesten umgeestert.

Wählen Sie Ihre Algenarten auf der Grundlage der Lipide Sie erzeugen wollen. Wählen Sie Ihre Algen auf die Nährstoffe, die Sie verwenden. Algen Biodiesel erfordert, dass Sie herausfinden, wie auf Seed, wachsen, nährstoff verwalten, Ernte, entwässern und trocknen Sie Ihre Algen in einem kommerziellen Prozess.

Wählen Sie Ihre Arten von Algen für Biodiesel, wie Sie oder andere beabsichtigen, das Öl von der Algenbiomasse zu trennen. Viele Unternehmen und Universitäten entwickeln Ölabscheidung Techniken, die Sie zugreifen können. Die häufigste ist eine Zentrifuge.

Algen für Biodiesel erfordert skalierbare Technologien im Handel, und alle beginnen im Labor wachsen Algen mit Photobloreaktoren.

Wachsende Algen für Biodiesel verlangt, dass alle Eingänge und Prozesse zu quantifizieren und wiederholbar werden. Arbeiten Sie Ihre Nährstoff Regime und Foto-Regime, wie Sie Ihr Wachstum Protokolle zu entwickeln.

Nährstoffbegrenzung, Temperaturschwankungen, Schwankungen Lichtstärke und Photoperioden, pH-Wert, und andere "Belastungen" können Algen Reaktion auszulösen.

Stickstoff Begrenzung wurde oft für "Induktion" Algen mehr Lipide zu produzieren wiesen.

Algen für Biodiesel ist ein "Motor" von schnell wachsenden Biomasse, die für Öle abgegriffen werden kann. Algen Biodiesel-Produktion hat viele Wertströme. Wachsende Algen für die Biodieselproduktion sucht "beeinflussen" Algen mehr Öl produzieren.

Die Ölproduktion in Algen "induziert" werden mit Variationen der Eingangsanforderungen produziert mehr mehrfach ungesättigte Fettsäuren-Säuren raubWasserVerschmutzung in den Prozess.

Algen für Kraftstoffe ist ein wichtiger Teil der großen Übergang des 21. Jahrhunderts in eine nachhaltige Industriegesellschaft.

Verwenden Algen-Photobioreaktor wachsen Kits zu wachsen und Forschung Algen für die Biodieselproduktion. Algen für Biodiesel ist in der Regel, indem die Öle aus der Algenbiomasse "verarbeitet" zuerst. Die "Presskuchen" verbleibenden Feststoffe sind eine gute Nahrung für Tiere und Fischfarmen.

Algen-Press-Kuchen mit den meisten Öle für Biodiesel entfernt lässt die Algen weniger ölig. Ideal für Ernährung Management Die "Öle" wurden entfernt, so dass die "Presskuchen" besser geeignet für die Tier-und Fischfutter.

Die "Presskuchen" ist reich an Aminosäuren, essentiellen Proteine, Antioxidantien, Vitamine und Spuren Öle hervorragend als Tier-und Fischfutter. Entfernt Die Öle werden dann durch Umesterung verarbeitet, um rutschig und stabil Algen Biodiesel zu produzieren.

Algen Biodiesel-Technologie reinigt Wasser, Produziert wertvolle Tier-und Fischfutter, Algen Biodiesel und produziert für den Einsatz in Dieselmotoren für Transport-und Energieerzeugungsmärkten.

Algen bieten große Chancen für die Herstellung Öle (Lipide) wegen ihrer hohen Eigen-Effizienz, und ihre Fähigkeit, Abfallprodukte, die als Nährstoffe nutzen.

Forscher und Unternehmen, haben ein besseres Verständnis darüber, wie Wachstum Umgebungen, wie zB mit der Photobioreaktor AlgaeToday PBR Algenzuchtsets, Algen Monokulturen, die hohe Gehalte an wertvollen produzieren wachsen können und Kontrolle - ausgewählt - organische Verbindungen von großem Wert für die Industrie.

Für Biokraftstoffe auf Algenbasis und Algen Biodiesel wachsenden Öl-reichen Algenstämme, die sich ansammeln Lipide sind der Schlüssel.

Einer der großen Pioniere in wachsenden Algen, die Photosynthese und die Erforschung, war Otto Warburg (1919), in Berlin, Deutschland. Gelang Warburg in wachsenden dichten Kulturen von Chlorella, und viele andere Arten (Taxa). Warburg war ein großer Visionär für die Verwendung von Algen als Ausgangsmaterial für Tier, Fisch-Feeds, und Biokraftstoffe.

Algen Biodiesel bietet viele Vorteile für den Transportmärkten. Erhältlich überall - organische Abfälle, die als Ausgangsmaterial ermöglicht ein Nährstoff Algen Biodiesel-Produktion in allen Ländern.

Algen für Biokraftstoffe verwendet die leistungsstarke Motor der Photosynthese zu tun, was industriell Pflanzen natürlich tun: recycle Kohlenstoff.

Algen Biodiesel ist klimaneutral. Kohlendioxid-CO2 in der Atmosphäre erfasst und von der Carbon-Fixierung mit Chlorophyll-a, und andere Pigmente Fahr Photosynthese in Proteine, Kohlenhydrate und Lipide (Öle) umgewandelt. Kohlenstoff wird "reduziert," wie Wasser "oxidiert" Fixierung von Kohlenstoff in Moleküle des Lebens.

Algen Biodiesel verwendet die Lipide für die Umesterung in stabile Biodiesel.

Der Konsum, oder brennende Algenbiomasse oxidiert die organischen Verbindungen, die Reform $CO_2$ in die Atmosphäre zurück. Kohlenstoffkreislauf für Algen ist Carbon Neutral - Keine neuen $CO_2$.

Die Treibstoffe Markt allein in den USA über $1800000000 Dollar pro Tag. Algen für die Biodiesel-Produktion würde Arbeitsplätze vor Ort und diverse Herstellung von Kohlenstoff-neutralen Biodiesel für Energie und wirtschaftliche Sicherheit einzuführen.

# Kapitel Sieben - Algenkulturtechniken

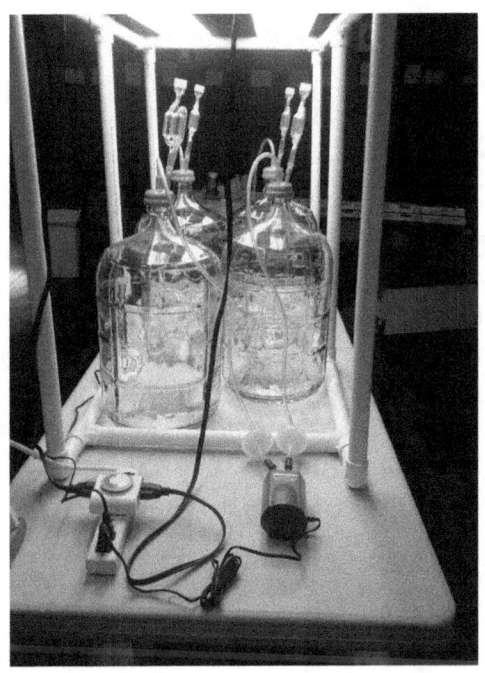

Growth-Rate Calculus:

Berechnung das Wachstum von Algen, folgt der Gleichung erster Ordnung: Gesamtzellvolumen pro Liter" dCV / dt = UCV, wobei u die "spezifische Wachstumsrate" und CV ist die

Wenn Sie über das Zeitintervall t1 und t2 Integrieren der log-linearen Wachstumsgleichung:  InCVt2 - wird InCVt1 = u (T1-T2) gefolgt.  Wo In Lebenslauf ist der natürliche Logarithmus des Volumens der Zellen pro Liter. Wird eine Zellkultur wird mit einer konstanten Rate wächst die Auftragung von ln Lebenslauf wird eine gerade Linie sein.

Eine einfache Methode für die Berechnung der Wachstumsraten:

Algen, wenn sie auf eine Wachstumskulturmedium als ein Impfmittel eingeführt, mit einem "Eingewöhnungsphase", wo Wachstumsraten werden zunächst gehemmt starten. Algenzellen werden "geschockt," wenn in eine neue Umgebung, und es gibt eine Zeit der Eingewöhnung, die manchmal auftritt für mehrere Tage, bis zu vielen Tagen, mit einer neuen Kultur in ein neues Wachstumsmedium eingebracht.

Algenwachstum, nach einer Eingewöhnungsphase, geben Sie einen "exponentiellen Wachstumsphase," wo Populationen vermehren sich rasch und mit einer steigenden Rate-of-Wachstum. Dieses exponentielle Wachstum von Algen-Phase ist, wo Algen Forscher finden ihre idealen Bedingungen.

Während dieses exponentielle Wachstum von Algen-Phase die "Anstiegsrate" in Zellen pro Zeiteinheit proportional zu der Anzahl der zu Beginn der Zeiteinheit enthaltenen Zellen. Die Bevölkerungswachstum der Algen folgt der Gleichung: dn / dt = rN Die Lösung dieser Gleichung ist bekannt: N (1) = N (0) e rt.

Messen Sie die Anfangspopulation von Ihrem Algen N (o), zu Beginn (T1), dann messen Sie Ihren Algenpopulation N (1) am Ende des Zeitraums. N (t) - was Sie produziert haben - wird gleich N (o), was Sie begann mit, mit einer Wachstumsrate (r) über die Zeitdauer (t).

Wenn Sie N (o) zu messen, N (1), im Laufe der Zeit zu lösen Periode T für Ihre Wachstumsrate (r).

Nach der exponentiellen Wachstumsphase verfügbaren Nährstoffe oder anderen Faktoren von großem Interesse für die Forscher sind "begrenzt," und die Wachstumsraten plötzlich langsam und bald aufhören. Wenn keine neuen Nährstoffe werden dann geliefert Algenkulturen gehen in einem rasanten Absturz.

Ein Biologe sagte einmal: "biologischen Systemen, wenn betont, entweder anzupassen oder zu sterben." Das ist sehr wahr mit wachsenden Algen. Frühe Algen Pionier wies darauf hin: "Wachstum ist begrenzt, durch das, was sie am meisten benötigt" - Blackman (1905).

Algenwachstum-Preise sind nicht das gleiche wie Algenbiomasseakkumulation.

Die Wachstumsraten sprechen Anzahl von Zellteilungen, und die Zahl der Zellen. Algenbiomasse liegt mit insgesamt "Masse" in

Bezug auf die Trockenmasse der vorliegenden Algen an den Beginn und das Ende besorgt.

Algen-"Yield" wird durch Messung der Impfmittel Trockenmasse in den Anfang der Algenkultur, und die Messung der Trockenmasse am Ende der Kultivierungsdauer bestimmt.
Balanced und Unbalanced Wachstum in Algenkultivierungs wird durch die Staats-und-Phase der Algenwachstum in Ihrem Photobioreaktor auftretenden bestimmt.

Die spezifische Wachstumsrate ist ein "Veränderungsrate" von Biomasse und wird durch die Größe des "anabole"-Prozesse (Photosynthese) und "katabolen"-Prozesse (Atmung) ermittelt: U = PR wobei U die "spezifische Wachstumsrate" und P ist die Photosynthese und R Atmung.

Die tägliche Sonnenzyklus der Bestrahlungsstärke erzeugt einen täglichen "Ungleichgewicht" der Photosynthese Verse Atmung. Dies stellt sicher, dass "unausgewogen" Wachstum ist der Grundstein des Algenwachstums. Dieses "unausgewogen" Wachstum ist eine große "Auslösemechanismus" in wachsenden Algen.

Algenarten, sind bemerkenswert für ihre Fähigkeit zu "akklimatisieren," um ihre Umwelt. Diese Eigenschaft wird durch Algen Grubber ausgenutzt, durch Wiederholung Bedingungen jeden Tag "Ausbildung" der Algen. Algen Taxa reagieren mit mehr vorhersehbares Ergebnis.

Algen folgt einem traditionellen 5-Phasen-Wachstumszyklus. Diese sind Akklimatisierung, Kompensationspunkt, exponentielles Wachstum, Sättigung, dann zusammenbrechen (wenn nichts anderes hinzugefügt). Diese 5 Phasen des Wachstums folgen eine klassische Kurve.

Akklimatisierung tritt auf, wenn Sie Ihre Wachstumsmedien mit einer kleinen Menge der reinen Arten zu impfen. Entschädigungen, tritt auf, wenn die Photosynthese die Energie von der Zelle für die Atmung benötigt wird, und die Wiedergabe überschreitet.

Exponentielles Wachstum tritt als nächstes alle verfügbaren Algen verbrauchen die Nährstoffe zur Verfügung.

Diese Phase ist von größtem Interesse Algen Forscher. Als Maxima erreicht ist, tritt ein Sättigungspunkt, wo die Wachstumsrate abnimmt. Die letzte Phase ist Kollaps.

Als Nährstoffe aufgebraucht sind, beginnen Mikroalgenzellen zugrunde gehen, und in der Regel beginnen zu sinken. Ohne die ständige Produktion von Lipiden, sind Zellen dichter und sinken.

Manipulation der Zellen, indem eine Variable (normalerweise Nährstoff) können Sie "trainieren" Ihr Algen an unterschiedliche Reiz reagieren.

# Frühe Arbeiten in Wachsende Algen

Algen wachsen Pioneer, Otto Warburg (1931), gewann den Nobelpreis für Forschung, und Erläuterung der Oxygenic Photosynthese, beschreibt Atemwege, mit der Grünalgen Chlorella. Warburg ist ein Held auf die phycological Feld.

Wachsende Algen und Mikroalgenkultivierung Labormethoden, findet seine Wurzeln mit Techniken, die in den späten 1800er Jahren entwickelt und frühen 1900er Jahren.

Die frühe Geschichte der Menschheit mit Algen wahrscheinlich begann, als paläolithischen Menschen geerntet natürlich vorkommenden Algen in Gezeiten-Pools und Teichen. In der Sonne getrocknet, würde Algen lebenswichtige Nährstoffe und Aromen alten Rezepten hinzugefügt haben.

Wachsende Algen in der modernen Ära begann in den frühen 1500er Jahren, in der Bucht von Tokio, und setzt sich bis heute in Japan und weltweit. Jüngste Fortschritte in der Algenanbaumethoden haben Algenkultivierungs (Algenkultur) in schnell wachsenden Märkten für Amino-bewegt Säuren, Proteine, Antioxidantien, Omega 3 - reiche Lipide und andere organische Moleküle.

Algen ist immer das Ausgangsmaterial der Wahl für die Versorgung Nutrazeutika-, Kosmetik, Aquakultur, und Biodiesel-Produkte.

Ferdinand Cohn (1850), die Gründungsväter der Bakteriologie, erfolgreich gehalten und schrieb über eine einzellige Flagellaten Form Chlorophyae. Haematococcus pluvialis in seinem Labor in Breslau, Polen  Haematococcus pluvialis ist eine wertvolle Algen für die Produktion von Astaxanthin.

Famintzin (around1871), St. Petersburg, Russland beschrieb seine Versuche wachsenden Algen in einer Lösung von ein paar gelösten anorganischen Salze.

Die meisten Algenwachstum auftritt, mit einem 12-Stunden und 12-Stunden-Photoperiode aus. Verlängerung oder Verkürzung der Verhältnis hat jedoch Auswirkungen auf die Zellphysiologie und Reaktion.  Wenn "Sonnenstunden" steigen die Alge wissen, dass der Sommer kommt und erhöht photosynthetischen Reaktion. Wenn "Sonne-Stunden verkürzt Alge reagieren auf" kommenden Winter "produziert mehr Lipiden.

Kulturtechniken gehören Impfen Ihre Wachstumsmedien, Messausgangsmasse, Einstellung Photoperiode.  Messen Sie alle Makro- und Mikronährstoffe, Metallionen, Vitaminen, sowie Lautstärke-Masse-Transfer von $CO_2$ und $O_2$ durch Ihr System. Messen Sie Ihre endgültige Masse, durch die Zeit T1-T2, berechnen Sie können Ihre Wachstumsrate.

# Kapitel Acht - Häufig gestellte Fragen zum Photobioreaktoren

### Frage: Was ist ein Photobioreaktor?

Ein Photobioreaktor (PBR) ist ein Bioreaktor mit einer Lichtquelle (n) stimuliert. Normalerweise Lichtquelle erzeugt Photosynthese-Raditiaon (PAR) Photonenenergie zwischen 400 nm und 700 nm Wellenlängen Aktiv. Eine grundlegende Photobioreaktor umfasst optische wachsenden Gefäße, Be-Eingänge, Ausgang Öffnungen, Bakterienfilter, Lichtquelle (n), Lichtautomat, und mechanische Struktur.

### Frage: Was sind Algen wachsen Kits?

Photobioreaktor Algen wachsen als komplette Kits PBR Hardware-Kits, die Sie zusammenzubauen.

Algen PBR Wachstums-Kits gehören ein Mechanische Rahmen, Beleuchtungssystem, das eine Nenn 200 micro-moles/m2/sec von PAR Licht erzeugt.

PBR-Kits gehören ein Heavy Duty-Timer und Leistungssystem, um Ihre Photoperiode kontrollieren (in der Regel 12 Stunden Hours-on/12-off) und abgesicherte Netzstecker. PBR Kits beinhalten eine Druckluftanlage von zwei (2) Luftpumpen, (4) Check-Ventile und (4) biologische Filter (0,22 Mikrometer), um Bakterien aus dem Belüftungssystem, bevor Sie Ihr Wachstum Schiffe mit vier (4) Pyrex Glasrohre für die Belüftung in den Wachstumsgefäßen zu entfernen.

**Frage: Warum bauen eine PBR Kit?**

Sie können eigene Materialien zu beziehen, und bauen Sie Ihre eigenen Photobioreaktor Kits. PBR-Kit wird alle grundlegenden Laborgeräte Sie Algen Taxa wachsen, in einer kontrollierten Umgebung mit niedrigen Kapitalkosten enthalten müssen.

Handelsübliche Qualität PBRs, auf dem Markt, sind in der Regel teuer und bieten viele Annehmlichkeiten und Funktionen wie Datenerfassungssysteme, die nicht unbedingt notwendig, wenn Sie "old-school" Techniken wie Titration Tests verwenden.

## Frage: Kann ich Skalieren Sie das PBR-Kits?

Ja. PBR-Kits sind skalierbare Kapazität, indem einfach mehr. Jedes Kit hat eine 8 Quadratmeter Stellfläche, und hat eine Kapazität von 80 Litern. Um das zu erreichen höhere Kapazitäten verwenden mehrere PBR-Kits. Wenn Sie 800 Liter Algen wachsenden Kapazität Gebrauch benötigen 10 Kits.

Large Scale Beispiel: (Hinweis: PBR Kits sind nur für Innengebrauch, geht davon aus, in diesem Beispiel einen Innen entsprechenden Arbeitsraum)

Ein Hektar umfasst rund 43.559 Quadratmeter. Mit Platz für Gängen (70% Verpackung eine Schicht) zwischen PBRs, können Sie 3812 Modell X-80-PBR-Kits für eine Produktionskapazität von 304.960 Liter. Installieren Algenbiomasseernte, mit gut organisierten Nährstoff, Wasser, Luft-Qualität und-Ort-Einsatz können je nach Geschick und Arten reichen.

Zum Beispiel werden (Ergebnisse variieren, aber zu Zwecken der Darstellung), kann ein Chlorophyta auf 1 Gramm pro Liter in gut geführten Kulturen geerntet werden. (Wesentlich höhere Dichten sind in der Literatur berichtet).

Ein Gramm / Liter / Growth-Zyklus würde eine Brutto (Trockengewicht) Algenbiomasse von 304.960 Gramm (304 kg) / Morgen / Wachstumszyklus. Ausbeute Mit 25 Tage / Monat in diesem Tempo Erträge, zum Beispiel 7.600 Kg pro Monat (91.200 kg / Jahr) der Algenbiomasse.

Die Wirtschaftlichkeit eines Großalgenkultivierungssystem, erfordert spezielle Management und Personal, ausreichend Nährstoffe, Wasser (und optional CO2)-Eingänge, Verarbeitung und Hardware für die Algenernte, Entwässerung und Trocknung. Wenn Sie möchten, dass die Hardwarekosten zu erkunden Groß kontaktieren Sie bitte unser Büro.

**Frage: Wie viel Biomasse kann ich wachsen mit PBR-Kits?**

Der englische Biologe Blackman, an der Wende des 20. Jahrhunderts, sagte: "Photosynthese ist ein Prozess begrenzt, durch das, was sie am meisten benötigt." Die Wachstumsraten abhängen, wie gut Sie haben ausgewogene alle Faktoren einschließlich der erforderlichen Nährstoffe (Makro und Mikro) gelösten Ionen und Vitamine.

Die Wellenlängen und Intensitäten der PAR-Licht, mit der Photoperiode setzen Sie Ihre Algenwachstum beeinflussen. Die Gesundheit Ihrer impfen, wenn Sie beginnen, und die Masse-Transfer von CO2 aus der Atmosphäre während des Wachstums (Belüftung bei der Zellatmung) in Form von gelöstem CO2 und O2, sowie der pH-Wert des Wachstumsmediums Management während des

Wachstums- Zyklus wird auch diktieren Ihre Wachstumsergebnisse.

Die Algenbiomasse (Trockengewicht) Wachstum von 1 Gramm / Liter, pro Zyklus ist wiederholbar, kann aber je nach Geschick, Taxa, und das Gleichgewicht der Systeme, wie Temperatur, pH-Wert und Nährstoffmischung gewählt. Niedriger oder höher liegen Algentrockengewicht Renditen Verwendung von PBR haben zwischen 5 und 10 Gramm pro Liter berichtet. Ihre Ergebnisse sind abhängig von der Wachstumsmedien, Taxa, PAR-Licht, Lichtperiode, und Geschick. Sie können einen wiederholbaren 3-4 g / l mit dieser Hardware zu erreichen.

**Frage: Wie viel Licht ist der PBR Kit produzieren?**

Photobioreaktor (PBR) Kits enthalten zwei (2) hocheffiziente Ballast T8 Leuchtstoffleuchten. Vier (4) Hocheffizienz-T8-Lampen sind bei 6500K spektrale Leistung enthalten. Können Sie die Zwiebeln mit unterschiedlichen spektralen Profile einfach mit der Größe T8 ersetzen. Nennleistung in der Höhe von 200 Mikro-Mole photons/m2/second von PAR-Scheinwerfer, die Sie nach oben oder unten durch unterschiedliche vertikale Beinsegmente, oder indem man das Licht in unterschiedlichen Höhen mit Kettenaufhängung enthalten einzustellen. Glühbirnen sind 20.000 Stunden ausgelegt der zu verwenden.

**Frage: Wie lange dauert es, bis die PBR Kits montieren?**

PBR-Kits sind einfach zu montieren und relativ schnell. Versammlung der komplette Kit dauert etwa zwei Stunden, wenn Sie langsam und stetig sind. Hinweis: wenn Sie bereit sind, zu impfen zerlegen die wachsenden Gefäßverbindungen und benutzen sind die Desinfektionsmittel enthalten (100% Non-Toxic) enthalten folgende Anweisungen, die verdampft, so dass Ihre Arbeitsflächen bereit für eine schnelle Verbindung, und Sie sind bereit, Ihre Starteralgen impfen sind Taxa.

**Frage: Was ist mit der Druckluftanlage in PBR Kit enthalten?**

PBR Kits beinhalten eine hocheffiziente Luftpumpsystem von zwei (2) Luftpumpen zusammengesetzt, (4) Check-Ventile, (4) 0,22 Micron Bakterielle Filter (eine für jedes Glas Wachsendes Schiff), mit 100% ungiftig Food- Grade Kunststoffschlauch (22 ') und Armaturen und vier (4) Pyrex Glasrohre für die Belüftung in das Algenwachstum Gefäße, nach der Teileliste in **Kapitel drei**.

**Frage: Wie kann ich steuern, Temperatur?**

Diese Algen-Photobioreaktor PBR-Kits sind für den Innenbereich konzipiert. Um die Temperatur des Photobioreaktor Wachstum Schiffe können Sie die Umgebungstemperatur des Laborflächen zu steuern, oder Sie können Heizelemente, wie Sie heißen Platten, vor Ort einzukaufen hinzufügen können. Meisten Algen wachsen gemäßigten Niveau um die 20 Grad C.

**Frage: Wie kann ich ernten Photobioreaktoren?**

Jedes Glas wachsenden Gefäß, 20 L oder 25 Liter Größe, (Kit enthält vier Schiffe) kommt mit einem Schnellspanner voller Dichtung Top-Stopper ausgestattet. (Verwenden Sie 100% ungiftig Lebensmittelqualität Kunststoff). Wenn Sie Ihr Wachstum Gefäße zugreifen möchten, entweder zum Laden Wachstumsmedien, die Entnahme von Proben, oder Ernte, entfernen Sie die Top-Stopper, und geben Sie Ihre Pipette, oder andere Glaswaren zu pumpen oder manuell extrahieren Sie Ihre Proben oder Ernte. Ersetzen Top-Stopper, wenn Sie Ihre Extraktion beendet haben. Ausschalten nicht Luftpumpen. Sie sollten 24/7 laufen.

**Frage: Wie kann ich rühren Kulturen?**

Die Mechanische Rahmung in der PBR-Kit Design enthalten ist, ermöglicht einen einfachen Zugang zu allen Komponenten. Auch wenn es eine sanfte Mischung pneumatisch von den Luftpumpen, können Sie ganz einfach "Swish" die Schiffe manuell geben dem Alge eine schonende, aber gut umrühren ohne Öffnen der Gefäße.

Frage: Brauche ich Spezialwerkzeuge, um die PBR Kits montieren?

Nein. Sharp Edge, Maßband, Schere und Plastikhandschuhe (empfohlen). Sobald Sie Ihren Rahmen können Sie die Teile mit PVC-Kleber kleben lokaler Herkunft zusammengestellt haben.

# Kapitel Neun - Quick-Guide, um Bau-Photobioreaktor

Photobioreaktor Algen wachsen Kits sind für Forscher, die Experimente durchführen wollen, konzipiert und müssen die Hardware, um Algen Monokulturen anzubauen.

Verwenden Sie Photobioreaktor PBR Algen-Kits gesteuert Photosynthese und Algenfarm für seine unglaubliche und wertvolle Proteine zu erstellen wachsen, Aminosäuren, Lipiden, Antioxidantien, Vitamine und andere erstaunliche Verbindungen

Photobioreaktor PBR Algen wachsen Kit - 80 Liter für den Anbau von Monokulturen von Algen.

übel in den Quellwasser.

Schritt: Montieren Rahmen aus PVC-Rohrleitungs Sie Quelle auf lokaler Hardware. Schnittlängen wie in Kapitel drei beschrieben.

Schritt zwei: Montieren Glasgefäße wachsen, mit 2-Loch-Stopfen (100% Lebensmittelqualität nicht-toxischen Kunststoff). Durch ein Loch schieben Kawumm (4 mm) fast auf den Boden des Glasgefäßes mit 2 cm über den Anschlag erstreckt. Das ist Ihre Lufteinlass Glasrohr. Zum Anfang das andere Loch, legen Sie eine Weide Curve die sich von der Anschlagbasis. Dies ist die "Exit" Ventil ermöglicht inneren Luftdruck aufzubauen, und einen konstanten Druck aus.

**Weide der Kurve verhindert, dass Bakterien aus kroch wieder in das Gefäß.**

Schritt Drei: Montieren Sie die Luftpumpen. Sie werden zwei Luftpumpen zu verwenden, aus einem Aquarium Versorgungs Haus, mit einem Splitter und zwei "Rückschlagventile." Du wirst Luft in zwei Wachstums Schiffe mit einer Pumpe pumpen. Von jeder Pumpe, legen inline ein Rückschlagventil, und vor jedem Schiff, werden Sie eine 0,22 um Bakterienfilter zu platzieren. Dadurch werden alle Bakterien oder Partikel aus der ankommenden Luft zu entfernen.

Schritt vier: Schließen Sie, unter Verwendung von 100% ungiftig Food Grade Schläuche, Bakterienfilter an den Lufteinlassrohr in Hole Einer der Stopper. Länge der Kunststoffschlauch ca. 22." Air, wird nun von einer Pumpe durch einen Splitter, um Wachstum Schiffe laufen gepumpt. Jedes "Bein" von der Pumpe "Splitter" wird ein Rückschlagventil und ein Bakterienfilter haben. Mit dem Schlauch, wie beschrieben, verbinden Sie das Downstream-Seite des Bakterienfilter an den Lufteinlassrohr am Loch Eine auf den Anschlag.

Fünfter Schritt: Montieren Sie die Leuchtstoffbeleuchtungskörper, und legen Sie sie auf dem Mechanische Frame. Stecken Beleuchtungseinheiten an eine Steckerleiste. Stecken Sie das Netz Streifen in ein Timer, und stecken Sie den Timer in die Wand Strom.

Schritt sechs: Dis-Rohre montieren und Glaswaren, und genießen in Sterilisator (Verdunstungs-Typ), bevor Sie die Gefäße mit Wachstumsmedien und Impfen zu laden.

Da haben Sie es, einen Photobioreaktor können Sie selbst zu bauen. Wachsen Algen für Gewinn, durch den Anbau von hoch geschätzten Arten.